If you want your nation to become holy before God, you need to read this book. It will wake up the reformer in you. You will be equipped to grab godly responsibility for regional transformation. I knew that I would be moved reading this, but something even more explosive happened. This book carries an ability to reset and realign us to our biblical mandate to disciple nations and cities, until God reigns freely in them. Cindy is a majestic storyteller who, with compelling honesty and authenticity, leads us into strategic, practical knowledge of the things that are important for us to wrestle with in the new era. Cindy is a permission-giver for you to enter into the role of stewarding dynamic change at a macro level.

EMMA STARK
Leader, Global Prophetic Alliance
& Power Church Glasgow, Scotland
Co-Leader, British Isles Council of Prophets
Author of *The Prophetic Warrior*

Cindy Jacobs has brought forth the research and revelation to bring reformation to the church. *Reformers Arise* gives divine directives for the church to fulfill Christ's command for us to pray and work for His kingdom to be demonstrated in every nation and His will to be done on earth as it is in heaven.

DR. BILL HAMON
Bishop of Christian International
Ministries Network (CIMN)
Author of *Day of the Saints*

Reformation means to bring change. For the church to bring change, we must first endure change. Cindy Jacobs paints a hopeful, encouraging picture of the reformation process God is doing in His church so that we can become His vehicle of transformation in the earth. Thank you, Cindy, for this prophetically inspired charge!

JANE HAMON
Apostle, Vision Church @ Christian International
Author of *Dreams and Visions*, *The Deborah Company*, *The Cyrus Decree*, *Discernment and Declarations for Breakthrough*

In this world there are many people who make an impact on those around them. Then there are others who also make an imprint. But there are only a few who, in addition to impacting and leaving an imprint, blaze a trail that leads multitudes to their destiny. Cindy Jacobs is a true gift from God and this book is a compelling manifesto that will envision, enlighten, and empower you to follow that trail. Read, be blessed, and go change the world!

DR. ED SILVOSO
Author, *Ekklesia: Rediscovering God's Instrument for Global Transformation*
Founder, Transform Our World

The message that Cindy Jacobs imparts through *Reformers Arise* couldn't be more relevant to the times we are living in. It is a word for this generation. This book will embolden you to be a change agent for the Kingdom of God as you pursue reformation in your sphere of influence.

DR. CHÉ AHN
President, Harvest International Ministry
Senior Pastor, Harvest Rock Church
Pasadena, California
International Chancellor, Wagner University
Founder, Ché Ahn Media

In the middle of Babylonian anti-God culture, the Lord raised up a reformer named Daniel who shook the whole system. Cindy Jacobs' book will give context and strategy to a last-days reformation reality, where in every place there will be testimonies of God's dominion and rule. With the authority of an outrageous life testimony, my spiritual mother leaves no room for the counsel of despair, nor the escapist abdication of history. Jesus is the Lord of history, and only the one who believes that statement will be able to become a reformer.

LOU ENGLE

Finally, more than a despairing assessment of eroding social and moral conditions! Cindy found the mind of God in a strategic plan that directs the body of Christ in practical considerations that *will* return our nation and the nations of the world to hope.

JIM HENNESY
Pastor, Trinity Ministries
Cedar Hill, Texas

REFORMERS
ARISE

REFORMERS
ARISE

YOUR PROPHETIC STRATEGY FOR
BRINGING HEAVEN TO EARTH

CINDY JACOBS

DESTINY IMAGE® PUBLISHERS, INC.

P.O. Box 310, Shippensburg, PA 17257-0310

"Promoting Inspired Lives."

Previously published as *The Reformation Manifesto* by Bethany House Publishers
Previous ISBN: 978-0-7642-0515-6

This book and all other Destiny Image and Destiny Image Fiction books are available at Christian bookstores and distributors worldwide.

Cover design by Eileen Rockwell
Interior design by Terry Clifton

For more information on foreign distributors, call 717-532-3040.

Reach us on the Internet: www.destinyimage.com.

ISBN 13 TP: 978-0-7684-6121-3
ISBN 13 eBook: 978-0-7684-6122-0
ISBN 13 HC: 978-0-7684-6124-4
ISBN 13 LP: 978-0-7684-6123-7

For Worldwide Distribution, Printed in the U.S.A.

1 2 3 4 5 6 7 8 / 25 24 23 22 21

This book is gratefully dedicated to
Peter and Doris Wagner.
Without their love and friendship, I never would be
where I am today in the ministry.

CONTENTS

NOTE FROM THE PUBLISHER

THIS IS A timely book. In fact, I believe it was written and released *before its time*. But that is often how prophetic things happen.

Originally released back in 2008, Cindy Jacobs' book outlines how a move of God is far more than energetic church services, prolonged gatherings, and evangelistic outreaches. Yes, those things are important *and* included, but a true move of God is seeing anointed men and women deployed into every sphere of society, carrying prophetic solutions that measurably impact entire systems and cultures. The move of God *moves* with you.

Cindy Jacobs is not only a friend, but she is a personal hero. I've followed her ministry for many years and consider her to be one of the leading prophetic voices on the Earth today. Why? Before she considers herself a prophet, she is a revivalist and a reformer. She doesn't desire to simply prophesy about transformation; she is one whom Heaven entrusts with the blueprints and strategies to see this transformation integrated.

Warning: This book will call you up higher. When I first read it, it challenged me. It will expand your thinking about what revival and awakening should produce in your life—and in the world around you. It will provoke you to consult the Lord on what part you are called to play in His agenda for nations—and that begins in your household. It starts in your school, your workplace, your sphere of influence.

Reformers Arise is a clarion call for you to take your place in the greatest move of God the earth has ever seen. It's time!

LARRY SPARKS
Publisher, Destiny Image
August 2021

FOREWORD

THEY SAY PEOPLE don't read forewords. I hope this case is different because this book is unique. *Reformers Arise*—what a title! This is a long-awaited blueprint for the people of God to take their place in the moment of America's greatest crisis since the Civil War. The move of God must combine desperate, focused prayer and specific action like never before because we are burning daylight.

Cindy Jacobs presents a prophetic blueprint for revivalists to become awakeners. Those who love the move of God, the secret place of His presence, and intercessory prayer are being called onto the center stage of a great cosmic conflict. It's time for God's lovers to become lovers who know how to war against systems and strongholds that are forming over us with unprecedented audacity. The new awakeners will move from acting as disjointed individuals into cohesive groups, ecclesias, contending for not only individual souls but discipling communities, systems, and nations. The devil has not been given authority over the entire earth. When Jesus returns, He will gather the nations and separate them into sheep and goats. Jesus said, "All power *has* been given to Me in heaven *and earth*." This is the hour when nations decide their fate. Our mission is to "make disciples of nations." Cindy calls us to rethink the witness of Christians to nations in the midst of a global reset.

A book like this is truly unique, because as a prophet and revivalist, Cindy is able to speak directly to the lovers who understand spiritual warfare. She speaks to those who love the presence of God, intimacy, and intercession, and she boldly calls them forth also as warriors who impact social structures. Cindy is recognized as a general in intercession whose experience in nations qualifies her to share an updated blueprint. It's no longer lovers or culture warriors, it's a merger producing a bride that is *"terrible as an army with banners"* (Song of Sol. 6:4 KJV). The people of God possess a unique DNA that positions them to walk in intimacy, war with intensity, and rule over the powers of darkness with authority. *Reformers Arise* breaks through the categorization that tends to happen in the church, where people pick their "camp," identify themselves by a certain stream or style, and settle there comfortably. We don't have the luxury to comfortably "settle down" while darkness is intentionally and aggressively shaping the course of world events under a new strain of end-time lawlessness.

For those lovers who say, "I don't get involved with the warfare stuff," Cindy writes chapters like "Legislating in the Heavens" which will call the lovers into real warfare prayer. Cindy speaks to those who say, "I'm a warrior so I only engage in spiritual warfare and don't need to be aware of what's going on in the world around me" by confronting this with teaching on the importance of economics, the great wealth transfer, and the role of finances in reversing the Genesis curse. For those who say, "My principal assignment is to have marketplace impact and not get involved with all of that 'spiritual' revival stuff," Cindy has written new chapters about the intersection of revival, awakening, and reformation as a convergence of forces that merge the marketplace with a stunning road map to reformation.

I often say that revival is personal; reformation is social. Everyone loves revival. Revival is like beautiful Rachel, while reformation is the less pretty older sister, Leah. In the Old Testament, Jacob desired to marry Rachel because she was a delight to behold, but God had a different plan. The great patriarch thought he married Rachel but woke up with Leah! Needless to say, he was disappointed. Little did he know that the sister he didn't want would produce for him the tribes that secured his legacy! They made Israel a great nation in the earth. Like Jacob, we love the fire, excitement, and passion of revival, but lasting gains and prosperity come from revived people producing reformation. Leah's sons tell us a story. *Reuben*—to behold or see God. *Simeon*—to hear God. *Levi*—to be joined to God's work in unity. And *Judah*—to rule over what you see and hear from Heaven as one unified witness. God is putting a demand on His people to arise and put their hand to the plow and boots to the ground in a great end-time demonstration.

Reformation calls revivalists to honestly evaluate the fruit of moves of God and recognize that spiritual awakening is essential, but it must result in the deployment of reformers into all spheres of society who translate the move of God into their place of jurisdiction and influence.

From the moment you dive into this book, be prepared to be challenged. But it's a "good" kind of challenge. It's a clarion call to recognize that revival and awakening must produce reformers. *You are holding this book* because you are a reformer who is being called to arise to your greatest hour of ministry. For the sake of your family, for the sake of your nation, for the sake of future generations—reformer, arise!

DR. LANCE WALLNAU
Bestselling author of *God's Chaos Code* and
God's Chaos Candidate
Founder and CEO of the Lance Learning Group

FOREWORD

***REFORMERS ARISE* IS** clearly a book for the Second Apostolic Age. I don't believe the church would have been ready for this book ten, maybe even five, years ago. But the church is ready now. One of Cindy Jacobs' many enviable qualities is her ability to discern, through the Holy Spirit, accurate timing. The book you have in your hands has the potential for igniting the fuel for some crucial booster rockets that will measurably advance the kingdom of God in our generation.

The Second Apostolic Age? For some this may be a new term. To the best of my calculations, the Second Apostolic Age began around 2001. What this means is that, for the first time in some eighteen hundred years, a critical mass of the body of Christ now recognizes the biblical government of the church based on apostles and prophets. We are now witnessing the greatest change in the way of doing church at least since the Protestant Reformation.

This new season has opened the way for the Holy Spirit to begin to reveal some things to church leaders that many were not previously ready to receive. Chief among these potentially history-changing fresh ideas relates to the theme of this book—reformation.

Reformation of what? Reformation of the societies in which we live. Cindy Jacobs is not alone in discerning this. She is not a voice crying in the wilderness. Rather, she is joining a chorus of cutting-edge leaders of the segment of Christianity that I like to think of as charismatically inclined evangelicals to proclaim that God's kingdom is coming here on earth as it is in heaven, and it is coming more rapidly than many have thought.

Many of us, me included, have for too long harbored a truncated view of the kingdom of God. We began by over-identifying the church with the kingdom and going on from there to imagine that our mission was to save souls and plant churches and let others worry about improving society. No longer! Jacobs is proclaiming a "reformation manifesto." We are also hearing terms such as *social transformation* and *city taking* and *cultural mandate* and *retaking dominion* and *ministry in the workplace.* We are much more aware than we have been that just being good Christians and living holy lives and praying harder and worshiping fervently and tithing our income—wonderful as that all certainly is—will not by itself be enough to reform society. We need to do more of that, but we also need to go hands on into society itself, and perhaps in the process even get our hands dirty.

I love the way Cindy Jacobs talks about things like the Great Commission. I used to think making disciples of the nations meant getting people saved and multiplying churches around the world. But Cindy brings it to a new level when she proposes that "Jesus wasn't looking to get people to change as much as He was looking to get kingdoms to change." She argues that history has shown that revivals per se have not produced sustained social transformation. Revival is not enough! We need a paradigm shift. When she moves into biblical economics, she even scolds St. Francis of Assisi! Why? Because he established the worldview that "poverty equals spirituality, and therefore wealth is sinful." In opposition to this, she advocates that we develop an "abundance mentality."

This is not typical religious language. We don't often hear things like this from our pulpits. One reason is that most of our "Spirit-filled" pastors have been taught that they should keep away from worldly things and that social concerns are usually marks of liberalism. But this is rapidly changing, and prophetic voices like that of Cindy Jacobs are speeding the process.

Reformers Arise is at the same time an exciting and a challenging book. It will thrill you, and it will disturb you. But through it I know that you will be hearing more and more clearly what the Spirit is saying to the churches these days. My prayer is that you will not only hear it but that you will allow it to penetrate your heart. If you do, you will join the ranks of those kingdom-minded and kingdom-motivated servants of God whom He longs to use to change our world!

C. PETER WAGNER
Presiding Apostle
International Coalition of Apostles

PREFACE

WE ARE SEEING the beginning of great moves across the earth today. Prophets are prophesying revivals and awakenings. The Lord is raising up a new breed of passionate leaders who are hungry for souls. 24/7 prayer movements are springing up on university campuses, and the fires of the precursers of revival are burning brightly in all-night prayer meetings.

I know that God is raising up great end-time revivalists. Prayer expeditions are being formed into the unreached parts of the earth. To me, there is no doubt that we are moving toward the return of the Lord. There are millions who still need to be saved, and I am crying out to the Lord for laborers to be sent into the harvest fields of the nations.

Why did I spend years of my life writing the book you are about to read? Because we need both revival *and* reformation. The Bible delivers out a clarion call in the Great Commission to *go and disciple and teach nations.*

Once we lead people to Christ, what then? After extensive study and prayer on this subject, I now understand that we are not only

11

meant to make disciples of individuals, but, like the Great Commission says, we are to make disciples of our nations.

Now, that is a big thought! We are to disciple people and train them to not only live good Christian lives but to be God's change agents in the earth. This means we are to go back to the beginning of the book and take back our original creation mandate.

I have preached for 45-plus years. More, if you count the times I taught Sunday school while my parents planted churches. I have been involved in revivals in Argentina, Brazil, Colombia, and other nations. I *love* revival! Even as I am writing this preface, pictures are flashing across my mind of the miracles I have seen—blind eyes opened and deaf ears opened supernaturally. I plan to see many, many more of those powerful sights! I love to preach in stadiums and see hundreds flood the altars.

However, after the lights go out and people have gone home, I have watched once-bright lights for the gospel dim. The very people who came to Christ supernaturally in those revivals now suffer challenges as their governments become oppressive. Even my nation, the United States that I love so much, has now become what many call a post-Christian nation.

Does that mean that I do not believe a massive revival and awakening is coming to America or other nations? Of course not! It will happen. I just know this army of the Lord must be taught to be *reformers* as well as revivalists. Can we dream one step beyond that to the transformation of our nations?

The Bible is the "how-to" manual to transform our nations. In order to get to that point, we need to learn how to *be* reformers and understand the biblical worldview. To fulfill our commission to *teach* nations, we must learn how.

This is a book of the "how-tos." We must study to show ourselves approved unto God. I invite you to really study this book. I believe that you are both hungry for revival and reformation. I long for you to not only read God's Word but learn to read God's world in the light of His Word.

Reformers throughout the centuries have been imprisoned, martyred, persecuted, and mocked, and yet kept going. They righted great wrongs, such as slavery and the right to vote for women. People have marched against injustice and stood against Jim Crow laws and racism.

We stand upon their shoulders. How can we fail to take the batons passed to us in our generation that have often fallen from lifeless hands?

Not on our watch!

CINDY JACOBS

NEW INTRODUCTION TO
REFORMERS ARISE

AS YOU OPEN the pages of this book, it is a fair question to ask, "Why do we need a new reformation?" Is this book about the reformation that began in the year 1517 when Martin Luther nailed his Ninety-Five Theses to the door of the Castle Church in Wittenberg, Germany?

Ironically, these "Theses" were not an attack on the church but a re-introduction of true repentance and a call to return to it. At that time, people were paying for indulgences, and, for the most part, justification by faith was not being taught, nor was it understood. Forgiveness of sin was a money-making venture. I believe that the Catholic Church today knows we need to be justified by faith.

Martin Luther was not looking to leave the Catholic Church but to reform it. From my study of church history, he did not know the ramifications of his postings as his hammer fell. This is often the case with reformers. You are reading this book because you are at the least curious about being a reformer, or you have heard others talk about going from revival to reformation. The generations of God's people have always been called to embody reformation.

We either haven't known how or were, at times, clueless the Great Commission was much broader than saving souls. It was also about disciplining nations.

Jesus' first sermon was clearly much broader than saving souls. He preached:

> *The Spirit of the Lord is upon Me, because He has anointed Me to preach the gospel to the poor; He has sent Me to heal the brokenhearted, to proclaim liberty to the captives and recovery of sight to the blind, to set at liberty those who are oppressed* (Luke 4:18).

You might further ask yourself, "What does reformation have to do with me? Why can't we just have revival?" One only has to search the history of past revivals to see revival is the *starting place* for us on the earth. Beyond that point, we need to be the hands and feet to see His will be done "on earth as it is in heaven."

Looking back at the history of civilization, there have been terrible atrocities, and some of them were done in the "name" or guise of Christianity. For instance, the belt buckles for the German Navy and Luftwaffe read, "Gott Mit Uns," or *God with us*. The Spanish Inquisition (1478–1834) was ostensibly formed to purge heresy from the nation. Among other things, it led to the expulsion of the Jews from Spain in 1492, following the Alhambra Decree. Between 40,000 and 100,000 Sephardic Jews were expelled during that time.[1]

Persecution of Christians around the world is on the rise today. As of January 17, 2020, 260 million Christians faced persecution. According to Open Doors, Christians remain one of the most persecuted faiths in the world.[2] The North Korean government tops the list of nations for their horrendous acts toward Christians.

Our societies in the United States and around the world badly need reforming. We are called to be salt and light to the world. That begs the question I feel I must ask as an American, "Why is America sliding so quickly into an anti-God society?" Many Christian leaders today are proclaiming, "We need both revival and reformation." Others are teaching about entering into every aspect of society as believers to bring the gospel. It is my opinion that my friend, Lance Wallnau, will be remembered as the modern-day voice for what is now known as "The Seven Mountains" of society.

1. Religion
2. Family
3. Government
4. Business
5. Education
6. Arts/Entertainment
7. Media

Reformers Arise looks into many of these areas. While there is a dawning realization that we are to make disciples of and teach nations, we also have a need to develop instruction manuals and teachings on the "how tos." How does one do that?

An important biblical tenet to understand in this process, taken from what Jesus called the greatest commandment: *"You shall love the Lord your God with all your heart, with all your soul, and with all your **mind**"* (Matt. 22:37). We must know God's Word and be able to read the world in its light. A good reformer knows how to do this and does it adeptly. For instance, if you are called into government, you should know what the Bible says about this mountain.

The Bible is the Creator's handbook or manual. He has established certain laws and His world operates on them. It doesn't matter whether or not we believe they are true. Ignorance or disbelief in His laws does not negate our being subject to them. For instance, take the law of gravity. We may not like the law of gravity, and we may not believe it is real; however, it will go into effect if we jump off a tall building. We can say all the way down to the ground that we do not believe in it and should not be subject to it, but we will certainly hit the ground hard!

Most of the body of Christ is very good at understanding revival. There are many, many books written on the subject. (Of course, each generation needs its own revival voice.) In like manner, as we strive to find our place on the seven mountains, we need to understand we need to be *informed reformers*. This book could be called *Informed Reformation*.

I am excited to say more and more people know the church needs to leave the building and change society. For that to happen, we need to take the time to study and learn to love God with our whole mind as Matthew 22:37 tells us.

You will note that in order to know what to reform, you need to understand where our societies have taken a turn away from God. This helps us know what needs changing and where we need to start in each mountain. In order to do so, we need to understand God's Word.

> *Be diligent to present yourself approved to God, a worker who does not need to be ashamed, rightly dividing the word of truth* (2 Timothy 2:15).

From there, we also get the importance of study or diligence in general. A reformer has to study.

I write about some of the great reformers in history in the following pages. My mentor, Peter Wagner, used to say, "If you don't know where you've been, you don't know where you are going!" You will learn about those who have gone before us and changed laws and brought justice. William Wilberforce was one of these. He spent his life to see slavery abolished in Great Britain in spite of poor health and living with pain. While he did not have good health, God gave him a convincing voice that convicted the heart of humankind. His voice rang out over and over in spite of the seemingly deaf ears and the seared consciences of Britain's lawmakers. Of course, we had terrible slavery in the U.S. as well.

As I studied the subject of reformation, something was kindled in my heart, soul, and mind—like a fire shut up in my bones. I want to see nations discipled and taught of the Lord, and I know that in order to do that I need to be a reformer. God calls us to not only convert individuals but to teach nations. As I mentioned, we need both revival and reformation.

It is my heart's cry for you to become a reformer. I pray God's truth will spring to life inside of you as you read these pages. I also desire for the words I have labored to write for you to give you knowledge on knowing what to reform.

God is raising up a new generation of on-fire, passionate leaders in every sphere or mountain of society. Part of this leadership will include revivalists who are burning with a passion to see souls won and thousands saved on college campuses, in schools, and the streets of cities around the world. God is also going to raise up an army of nation-shaking reformers who will march across the face of the earth with a new holiness movement.

No matter whether you are young or old; short or tall; in need of shedding a few pounds; red, yellow, brown, black, or white—God has called you to a fulfill a destiny and purpose greater than yourself in your generation. It is time we stand together with the reformers of old and bring His light to the world.

Will you join me in learning how? Let's begin!

CINDY JACOBS
Dallas, Texas

Chapter One

PERSONAL REFORMATION

I HARDLY FELT like a reformer standing with my friends in the misty afternoon weather in Wittenberg, Germany, yet something stirred deep within my heart as I looked at the sign on the wall proclaiming the museum we had entered was once the home of Martin Luther.

It was just a day or so after a conference I had spoken at in Berlin, and our German host, Reiner, had agreed to take a few of us sight-seeing. As we walked down a corridor, I was somewhat shocked that Lutherhalle, the museum of Luther's life and teachings, was even open on Easter Sunday afternoon. In fact, to the people in charge of the building, it seemed like any other day rather than the one that commemorates the resurrection of Jesus Christ.

Advancing through the halls of the former monastery turned home to Luther and his beloved wife, Katie, the flicker of emotion that I had sensed as I first stepped onto the ancient stone floor increased. The longer we walked and read the history of the amazing cultural changes produced by this man's life, the more my wonder grew. I kept exclaiming to our group, "Look at this!" and "Read this!" I began to wonder what was stirring inside me. Why was I feeling like this?

Why indeed. You see, on those musty walls were living truths that are as relevant today as they were five centuries ago when Luther prayed while walking those same hallways.

Each time I read Luther's words my mind would bring up parallels between the need for nations to return to godliness today and Luther's reformation.

For one, Luther used the arts and music. He revolutionized church culture by writing songs that all the people could sing together in their common language. Up to that time there had not been congregational singing in church services. Worship became a key to the Reformation.

My heart caught fire as I read the lines from one of Luther's most well-known hymns, "A Mighty Fortress Is Our God":

> *A mighty fortress is our God,*
> *a bulwark never failing.*
> *...Did we in our own strength confide,*
> *our striving would be losing;*
> *Were not the right Man on our side,*
> *The Man of God's own choosing:*
> *Dost ask who that may be?*
> *Christ Jesus, it is He;*
> *Lord Sabaoth, His Name,*
> *From age to age the same*
> *and He must win the battle.*
> *...That word above all earthly pow'rs,*
> *No thanks to them, abideth*
> *The Spirit and the gifts are ours*
> *Thro' Him who with us sideth:*
> *Let goods and kindred go,*
> *This mortal life also;*

The body they may kill:
God's truth abideth still,
His kingdom is forever.

Even though this hymn was written in 1529, it still touches me and thousands of others in the midst of life's battles—God will prevail!

As we came to the last rooms of the museum I realized that large numbers in whole cities had been impacted by this reformation. It shook Germany as well as all of Europe. All of a sudden, I felt like a volcano was going to erupt inside me.

Rushing out of the museum into the damp, chilly afternoon, I could no longer contain myself. With my face to the wall, tears erupted from the depths of my being as I moaned, "O God, I'm so sorry, I'm so sorry! My generation has utterly failed You! O Lord, what is wrong with us?"

You see, at that moment I had a revelation that the very elements needed to change the face of the earth had been before our eyes for centuries, and yet somehow we have been impotent to fulfill the Great Commission.

Tears flowed down my face and mingled with the drops of rain as I groaned, "Eighty-three million people in Germany and only 1.5% of them are believers. O God, what is wrong with us? I'm so sorry, God. How could we have let this happen on our watch?"

At last I walked away, feeling quite shaken at what I had just experienced. I knew that I had travailed deep in my soul for the nation Luther had loved—the land of the Gutenberg Bible, the first printed German translation of God's Word.

As we continued to wander the streets of Wittenberg, talking about the need for reformation fires to once again blaze in this nation and the nations of the world, we looked for the doors that bore the revolutionary words Luther had penned. The famous Ninety-Five Theses that Martin Luther nailed to the Castle Church doors are now forever immortalized with a bronze replica of the papers in the same place he originally posted them.

While we walked, we talked about the problem of abortion in Germany. After East and West Germany were reunited, legalizing abortion became a heated debate. Abortion during the first trimester had been legal in East Germany since 1972, while in West Germany it had not. A compromise was finally struck in 1995, legalizing abortion in the first trimester as long as the woman received counseling first.[1] Since that time, Germany has seen approximately one hundred thirty thousand babies killed through abortion each year[2] with roughly 15 percent of all German pregnancies ending in abortion. In the city of Berlin that percentage is about 28 percent.[3] German feminists had rallied together, raised their voices, and marched through the streets, influencing the legalization of abortion in the reunited republic.

This led to my musing, how come the feminists have more courage than we Christians? Why aren't we seeing righteous laws put into place? Why are we so weak to change things in our culture when others are bold and passionate about their causes? Why don't we do something?

"Let's agree in prayer that abortion will again be made illegal in Germany," I said aloud to the others.

All agreed, and we stopped to hold hands and pray on the spot. Then we continued down the same path that Luther would have taken to the cathedral.

By late afternoon, we found what we had been seeking—the bronze memorial on the cathedral door—the document written by the radical reformer who shifted a whole nation with his words. We quietly joined hands and prayed that God would use us, among others, to help start a movement that would one day result in abortion being abolished in Germany. In addition, we cried to the Lord for the youth of Germany to rise up and see their whole nation saved.

As we finished our prayers, the notes of "A Mighty Fortress Is Our God" resounded from the large bell tower next to the cathedral. It was as if God Himself was saying, "Amen! About time that prayer was prayed. Now go do it!"

We stood in awe. The pealing of the music was so loud it shook us to our core. It was a supernaturally empowered moment. However, as powerful as that hallelujah-chorus-type experience was, God had prepared a stronger exclamation point to our adventure that none of us could have orchestrated.

As we turned to leave, a couple who appeared to be in their early sixties was in the process of taking pictures. We were surprised to see them, as no one had been on the streets but us. It had been such dreary weather most of the afternoon, not a typical time for tourists to be out taking pictures, especially as dusk approached.

The husband prepared to shoot a photo of his wife, and I felt a nudging of the Holy Spirit to offer to take their picture together. (Actually, I was going to offer Reiner, thinking I couldn't take it without cutting their heads off in the shot.) The gentleman thanked us and said that his wife, who was a Lutheran, had wanted her photo taken in front of the famous Wittenberg door.

After the photograph, I introduced our group—Laura Allred, Reiner Huss, Ben, and me. To our amazement, he introduced himself as a pro-life lawyer from Chicago. He was on vacation from acting as counsel on cases before the U.S. Supreme Court to overthrow abortion! We stumbled over our words as we excitedly shared with him what we had just prayed and how his being there at that moment was such a confirmation to us that one day abortion would again be illegal in Germany. After our conversation, we all prayed together and for each other.

Needless to say, we hardly needed a car to drive home—we were so excited we felt like we were flying! One day abortion will be illegal in Germany. It is comforting to know that even now God is raising up a new generation both there and across the face of the earth of radical, zealous reformers and revolutionaries who will see righteousness prevail in their nations.

Fanning the Flames of Reformation

As I have traveled around the world, I have had the opportunity to talk with people from all generations, who, though separated by age, are not separated by heart and passion.

They want to be used of God to change their nations.

How does one become a reformer? If you're like some people, it's like a bicycle cresting a hill, gradually gathering momentum as the need for change is clarified in your heart and you realize God wants you to do something about it. Usually there comes a catalytic moment that opens your eyes to the need for change. Martin Luther had one of these moments as a young man in the midst of a thunderstorm. It was a Damascus road experience for him, only he was on the road to Erfurt. It took place July 2, 1505, when Martin was twenty-one years old.

He was just a few miles from home when lightning struck so close to him that it knocked him off his horse. There must have been something supernatural in this wake-up call, because it caused him to cry out, repent of the sins of his youth, and vow, if his life was spared, to become a monk. Martin was true to his word. On July 17, 1505, he joined an Augustinian hermitage in Erfurt—which was the most rigorous of the seven monasteries in the area—instead of returning to law school.

His father was furious at his decision because he had sacrificed to put him through school to become a lawyer. (However, Martin was going to need the skills of a lawyer when later called before the religious councils of the day.)

Luther became a priest in 1507 and began teaching at the University of Wittenberg in 1508. In 1512, he received his doctor of theology degree, but he still couldn't get away from feeling he was a miserable, unworthy sinner. In 1515, he began a series of lectures on the books of Romans and Galatians. Somehow in the process of studying and meditating on the subject matter, God gave him a revelation that he summed up in one verse: "*The just shall live by faith*" (Rom. 1:17).

Regarding this experience, Martin Luther wrote:

> At last, meditating day and night, by the mercy of God, I...began to understand that the righteousness of God is that through which the righteous live by a gift of God, namely by faith. Here I felt as if I were entirely born again and had entered paradise itself through the gates that had been flung open.[4]

Through this revelation, Martin Luther saw that it was not so much about what he did as about what Jesus had done. Luther experienced a personal reformation that would change his world. It was only months later that Luther nailed his Ninety-Five Theses to the door of Castle Church.

What he had read in the book of Romans were the words of another young lawyer, the apostle Paul, who had also been dropped to his knees by a flash of light from heaven. As he traveled on the road to Damascus with letters granting him the authority to bring the followers of Jesus back to Jerusalem in chains, a flash of light knocked him to the ground, and he had a similar reformation. He met Jesus face to face and realized his zeal was misplaced. He later reported to the Galatians what was said of himself: *"He who formerly persecuted us now preaches the faith which he once tried to destroy"* (Gal. 1:23).

The point that I want to make here is that each of us needs to have a personal reformation. Of course, the first step is asking Jesus to forgive your sins and inviting Him to be the Lord of your life. However, for those who have become world-changing reformers, there also comes a moment in time—like my visit to the Luther museum—when one becomes passionately involved with wanting to right wrongs.

For many years I felt that my role in righting wrongs was to be entirely on a one-to-one basis. By this I mean that I would see a hungry person and feed him or her (which I still believe in doing on a regular basis) or pray for a hurting person. All this was good, but I wasn't engaging my mind on a macro level. My worldview needed to be refocused. I needed to reform my thinking regarding my role as a believer. My lens had been framed by the way I looked at God's commission to me personally from His Word.

My worldview began to shift in 1985, when God told me that whole nations could be healed.[5] Frankly, I didn't even realize they could be sick. Part of my problem was that I had been educated with a worldview based in Western/Greek thinking. The Greco-Roman—or Western—worldview is based on the individual and a separation of the supernatural from the natural.

How did this thinking affect my actions? First of all, I thought I was only responsible to God for living a godly life rather than being a steward of my nation, its laws, and society in general. I was bound by individualistic thinking. God doesn't only think individually but also in terms of nations and kingdoms. Biblical thinking is corporate in nature.

We can see this theme in the Old Testament reflected in Adam and Eve's sin in the garden, initiating the fall of all humanity (see Gen. 3:1-8); the sins of the ancestors affecting the generations "down line" (see Exod. 20:4-6); the sin of Achan causing the military defeat at Ai (see Josh. 7); the prophets of Israel condemning exploitation of the poor and social injustice (see Amos 5:7-15); and the fact that Israel as a nation went into captivity. This theme is also pervasive in the New Testament from its emphasis on how we are not only individuals but members of the body of Christ (see 1 Cor. 12) to its teaching that our responsibility extends to seeing the kingdom of God manifested in our nations.

Our worldview is critical to how we live our lives. German social economist Max Weber used terminology related to worldview in his analysis of the relationship between a people's belief system and their level of prosperity or poverty.[6] Our worldview should come through Scripture—it should be biblical. My worldview massively shifted one day when I was reading what many call the Great Commission:

> *Go therefore and make disciples of all the nations, baptizing them in the name of the Father and of the Son and of the Holy Spirit, teaching them to observe all things that I have commanded you; and lo, I am with you always, even to the end of the age* (Matthew 28:19-20).

As I read these verses, my eyes were suddenly fixed on the words "make disciples of all the nations." *Wait a minute!* I thought. *Doesn't that mean individuals?* All my life I had read that passage as a mandate to go out and win souls for Christ. (Please understand, I am by no means negating the need to evangelize each individual personally.)

Grabbing my concordance, I looked up nations and found that the Greek word used is *ethne*, from which we get *ethnic*. The corresponding Old Testament word is *mishpachah*, most often translated *families* (as in tribes or clans). The point is that God cares about our social connectedness, our cultural backgrounds, where we come from, what our places of origin are. God also cares about how we function together in society—how our laws promote (or go against) justice and righteousness, and how we make decisions that affect all of us (politics). In Bible times, your tribe, clan, group of clans, or city-state was your "nation." However, today the main social/political organizations are nation-states, huge conglomerates of people brought together by social and economic forces that very often work against the tight cohesion found in tribes, clans, and city-states. Therefore, while I respect the position heralded in mission literature that the "nations" of Matthew 28:19 are strictly "ethnic groups," in this book I accept that God also meant geopolitical states and nations as they are drawn on our maps today.

With my heart thundering, I returned to my Bible and read further down, stopping at the words *"teaching them to observe all things that I have commanded."* Teaching who to do what? I mused. And then I saw it! What I saw reformed my worldview of my mandate as an individual on this earth. This is the revelation:

> **We are called to disciple whole nations and teach them to observe everything God commanded.**

My next thought after that stunning revelation was, *Is there any nation on the face of the earth where believers have been successful in*

30

seeing their whole nation discipled and their society governed by God's Word? I know some have tried, but I could not think of one that had succeeded.

The thought gripped me. Christianity has been around for two thousand years. Millions of Christians have read those words in Matthew 28. We have the power of the Holy Spirit in our lives, and yet societies are deteriorating around us. What is the problem? How could there be roughly 2.2 billion Christians on the face of the earth today and the major problems of sin, poverty, and disease still plague the planet? Why haven't we figured out solutions to these problems? I understand that these are huge issues, but we have an even bigger God!

To be totally transparent with you, one of my major struggles in writing this book was that I wondered how I could engage ordinary believers into wanting to disciple their nations to become reformers themselves. We will never see righteousness come to our planet without a personal reformation as to our role as Christians.

First of all, we need to care for our nations like Jesus cares for them. He loves the nations of the earth—He created them! God cares that people are hungry, that babies are being aborted. Not only that, but on the macro level, He has the answers to systemic poverty, the AIDS epidemic, and other massive, mind-boggling problems. He wants to involve each of us in creating solutions and will show us what we need to do to be reformers and revolutionaries in our society.

One of the most powerful ways to learn is by looking at the lives of others who have gone before and have had a major impact on their nations.

ARE YOU WILLING TO BE THE CHANGE YOUR WORLD NEEDS?

It was 1942 in Nazi Germany. Hitler was in the midst of ravaging the youth of the nation with his lust for conquest and war. The turning point for one young woman named Sophie Scholl, a student at the University of Munich, was a sermon by the Bishop of Muenster, Clemens Galen. (This goes to show the importance of pastors being bold to cry out against injustice from their pulpits!)

Bishop Galen spoke against the emerging euthanasia policies of the Third Reich. Hitler was, with and without parental or familial permission, "euthanizing" the mentally retarded and infirm. It was in line with his Aryan eugenics plan—Hitler and his top aides believed that the mentally ill and the developmentally delayed would contribute negatively to the "bloodlines" of Europe.[7] More than one hundred thousand were killed in what was called the "T-4" program. Bishop Galen declared this selective breeding "was against God's commandments, against the law of nature, and against the system of jurisprudence in Germany."

Sophie and her brother, Hans, were horrified by these practices. They and some of their fellow students felt compelled to distribute Galen's sermon in pamphlet form at the University of Munich even though it was illegal to do so.

At this juncture of the war, Sophie and Hans, who had both been part of the German Youth League, had become disillusioned with Hitler and Nazism. They, along with Alexander Schmorell, banded together to write leaflets of resistance calling for the overthrow of Hitler. Hans (twenty-four) and Alexander (twenty-five) were medical students, and Sophie (twenty-one) was studying to be a nurse.

A university professor, Kurt Huber, who was forty-nine, along with three other medical students, Willi Graf, Jürgen Wittenstein, and Christoph Probst, also became involved. Together they called their group "The Society of the White Rose." The movement patterned their idea of nonviolent resistance after that of Gandhi and his followers, who were fighting against racial discrimination against Indians in South Africa. Their pamphlets called for social justice as well as a return to democracy in Germany.[8]

Most of the members of the White Rose had been in the German army and saw firsthand the atrocities done to the Jews by the Nazis. Their protest pamphlets described the mass executions and human rights violations in the concentration camps. This kind of writing was, of course, forbidden by Nazi law.

Hans Scholl had been marked to speak out against the treatment of the Jews by something that had happened during his service in the German army. His catalytic heart change from a Nazi to a reformer came when he saw a young Jewish woman who was forced to dig trenches. He thought at that moment, *There, but for the grace of God, I could have been—or one of my sisters.* Hans reached down to give her a flower and food, but she resisted. He knew that she was destined for one of the concentration camps and almost certain death. The event so struck his heart that when he returned to medical school, he devoted his young life to his views and his faith in God.[9]

This was Hans' "road to Damascus experience." He would never be the same. Then when the gauntlet was thrown down by Bishop Galen, he could not remain silent. History was about to be made by a handful of radical believers. Their method at first was to write leaflets and send them anonymously to people all over Germany. They would travel to different parts of the country on the weekends and take names and addresses from telephone directories. They concentrated on university professors and bar owners—people of influence who were open to discussing new ideas.

Then came the news of the defeat of the Nazi army at Stalingrad. Hundreds of thousands of Germans were killed in that battle, most eighteen- and nineteen-year-old boys. Some ninety-one thousand other Germans were taken as POWs—only six thousand of which would eventually make it back home. The vast majority of these POWs died of malnutrition, disease, and lack of medical care in Russian concentration camps.[10]

I have personally stood with pastors from the area on the mountain where the greatest fight of that battle took place. The Russians were fierce fighters, and their city was horribly decimated. Their losses were unimaginable, yet somehow they held back the German attack.

The news of the defeat emboldened the seven leaders of the White Rose to believe that the time to end the war was upon them. On the nights of February 4, 8, and 15, 1943, the group painted anti-Nazi slogans at twenty-nine different sites in Munich. They wrote, "Down with Hitler!" "Hitler the Mass Murderer!" and "Freiheit! Freiheit! Freiheit!" (Freedom! Freedom! Freedom!). Their signboards were the sides of buildings where they drew crossed-out swastikas.

They earnestly believed the youth of Germany could overthrow the evil regime Hitler had built. They produced about nine thousand copies of their sixth leaflet entitled "Fellow Fighters in the Resistance"—which this time had been drafted by Professor Huber—and sent it out on February 16 and 18. It read:

> Shaken and broken, our people behold the loss of the men of Stalingrad. Three hundred and thirty thousand German men have been senselessly and irresponsibly driven to death and destruction by the inspired strategy of our World War I Private First Class [referring to Hitler].

...The name of Germany is dishonored for all time if German youth do not finally rise, take revenge, smash its tormentors. Students! The German people look to us.[11]

All these actions put the Gestapo into a frenzy without a clue as to who the culprits were. They could not figure out how this resistance could be thriving. Finally, Hans and Sophie were caught throwing tracts off of a third-floor balcony at the University of Munich.

After their arrest on February 18, 1943, the Nazis moved with stunning speed against the three initially arrested—Sophie Scholl; her brother, Hans; and Christoph Probst. Just four days later, they were put on trial for treason. After the justice, Roland Freisler, ranted and raved at them, it was clear that he could never conceive how children who grew up in nice German homes could have committed what he felt were such atrocities against the Third Reich and the Fatherland.

Sophie Scholl shocked everyone in the courtroom when she answered Freisler, "Somebody, after all, had to make a start. What we wrote and said is also believed by many others. They just don't dare express themselves as we did." Later in the proceedings, she told him, "You know the war is lost. Why don't you have the courage to face it?"[12]

Robert and Magdalene Scholl, Sophie and Hans' father and mother, tried to come to their children's defense. Magdalene tried to enter the courtroom, telling the guard, "But I'm the mother of the accused." The guard responded, "You should have brought them up better," and refused her entrance. Robert Scholl forced his way into the courtroom, and as the guards held him, he told the court he had come to defend Hans and Sophie. The judge had him thrown out, but not before the entire courtroom heard him shout, "One day there will be another kind of justice! ...One day they will go down in history!"[13]

I cannot conceive of the pain these parents went through. At this moment I am thinking of my own two children, now thirty and twenty-six, trying to put myself in these parents' place—oh, the anguish!

The court pronounced the judgment—death by guillotine. The sentence was carried out that very afternoon.

While they waited for execution in Stadelheim prison, the guard allowed Sophie and Hans to see their parents one last time. They were both brave and conveyed their affection as well as their conviction. Hans asked his parents to give his regards to his friends, whom he named. For a moment he broke, but then faced them with a smile.

Sophie's last visit was so poignant that I want to give you the written account from *A Noble Treason* by Richard Hanser:

> Then a woman prison guard brought in Sophie.
>
> She was wearing her everyday clothes, a rather bulky crocheted jacket and a blue skirt, and she was smiling. Her mother tentatively offered her some candy, which Hans had declined.
>
> "Gladly," said Sophie, taking it. "After all, I haven't had any lunch!"
>
> She, too, looked somehow smaller, as if drawn together, but her face was clear and her smile was fresh and unforced, with something in it that her parents read as triumph.
>
> "Sophie, Sophie," her mother murmured, as if to herself.
>
> "To think you'll never be coming through the door again!" Sophie's smile was gentle. "Ah Mother," she said, "Those few little years..."

Sophie Scholl looked at her parents and was strong in her pride and certainty. "We took everything upon ourselves," she said. "What we did will cause waves."

Her mother spoke again: "Sophie," she said softly, "remember Jesus." "Yes," replied Sophie earnestly, almost commandingly, "but you, too."

She left them, her parents, Robert and Magdalene Scholl, with her face still lit by the smile they loved so well and would never see again. She was perfectly composed as she was led away. Robert Mohr (a Gestapo official), who had come out to the prison on business of his own, saw her in her cell immediately afterward, and she was crying.

It was the first time Robert Mohr had seen her in tears, and she apologized. "I have just said good-bye to my parents," she said. "You understand..." She had not cried before her parents. For them she had smiled.[14]

Christoph Probst, the third young man, twenty-three years old, faced death alone. No one in his family knew he was going to die. His wife was in the hospital having just given birth to their third child. After a Catholic priest visited with him and baptized him, Christoph said, "Now my death will be easy and joyful."[15]

The three of them, after being allowed a brief visit, met their death with dignity and victory. Observers commented that Sophie walked to her death without flinching. Hans cried out just before they cut off his head, "Long live freedom!" A single rose was found in his pocket, no doubt as a final statement that what they had done to free Germany would outlive their deaths.

And freedom did prevail in Germany. Hitler committed suicide, and the invincible Third Reich was overthrown. The stalwart stance these young people took for their beliefs shook a nation and is still impacting lives around the world through print and media today.

Traudl Junge, one of Hitler's private secretaries, spoke with regret of her service to the Nazis when she learned of Sophie Scholl after the war:

> One day I was walking past the memorial in Franz Josef Street to Sophie Scholl, a young girl who opposed Hitler, and I realized that she was the same age as me and that she was executed the same year I started working for Hitler. At that moment I really sensed that it was no excuse to be young and that it might have been possible to find out what had been going on.[16]

STANDING FOR FREEDOM

During the same visit to Germany in which I went to Wittenberg, Reiner told me about the Society of the White Rose. When I heard the story, and he suggested that we buy some white roses to give away during the conference at his church, I knew that God wanted us to start a whole new movement of Christian youth who would help reform their nation. The Southstar Church—where our conference was held—is housed in a beautiful old cathedral that used to be Hitler's military chapel. From that chapel, he would challenge his young troops to pledge their lives unto death to him and the Third Reich. After I preached that night about taking up the cause to see legalized abortion overthrown in Germany, it seemed only appropriate that we pass out white roses.

So at the end of the message, I stood and simply said these words while I held up a white rose: "Who will pick up the mantle of Sophie and Hans Scholl and help start a new move of God in this nation?"

It was as if thunder struck in that beautiful old cathedral. While we stood in the exact place where Hitler called a generation to serve his own blood lust and racist ideologies, a new movement was born. Grown men—affectionately known as "German Oaks" because of their lack of emotion—were surging forward and taking a white rose with tears in their eyes. Younger men and women were no different as they answered the same call.

Sweet justice, don't you think? I wonder if God let the cloud of German witnesses who are in heaven look down from His balcony that night to see what was happening. I believe this reformation will have double the anointing the last one had to reform their nation.

God is looking for more reformers. Are you willing to join us?

REFORMER'S PRAYER

O God,
Please use me to change the nations of the earth. Use me to change and reform my nation. I give myself to You.
In Jesus' name. Amen.

Signature _____

Date _____

Chapter Two

CONNECTING THE GENERATIONS

AS I STOOD on a windswept hill in Herrnhut, Germany with a small group of friends, I could hardly believe where I was and wondered about those before us who might have stood praying in this same spot. For many years I had heard of the famous one-hundred-year prayer meeting of the Moravians, and now I stood in the village where it had all begun. The visit was unplanned in my agenda, but totally planned by God. It was another piece of the reformation puzzle He was putting together in my soul.

We had made a stop over in Prague, Czech Republic, as we traveled through five European nations on our way to Poland for another conference. Our friend Lee Ann said to another friend JoAnna and me, "How would you like to go to Herrnhut on the way to Poland?" We only had to pray about one second before we shouted, "Yes, let's go!"

We were able to make tour arrangements with a descendant of one of the original praying Moravians, and off we went.

The village of Herrnhut was established in 1722 by Hussite refugees from Moravia—thus the name "Moravians"—fleeing persecution from the Counter-Reformation. Herrnhut means "The Lord's

Watch." The land was owned as part of the estate of Count Nicholas Ludwig Zinzendorf, who was twenty-two years old at the time he granted them asylum.

Zinzendorf purchased the land from his grandmother, Baroness von Gersdorf, and he established the village of Berthelsdorf on part of it. Soon afterward he formed a group he called the "Band of Four Brothers" with three of his friends—Johann Andreas Rothe, pastor at Berthelsdorf; Melchior Schaffer, pastor at Gorlitz; and Friedrich von Watteville, a friend from boyhood. They met frequently for prayer and study and proceeded to stir up a small revival in the region. They printed and distributed large quantities of Bibles, books, tracts, and collections of hymns.

After the group's establishment, Zinzendorf moved to Herrnhut with his wife and children. The Moravians entered his life during this fertile time, but once the Moravians had escaped the external pressures of their previous home, strife and division tore at them from within. They had been driven fanatical by persecution and seemed to argue about everything. At one point they even turned on Zinzendorf and Rothe and denounced them as the Beast of the Apocalypse and his False Prophet.

Being a man of God, Zinzendorf stood steadily against the storm. Finally, on May 12, 1727, the community reached a turning point when Zinzendorf gave a three-hour address on the blessedness of Christian unity. The congregation fell into repentance, and a revival swept the village. The summer of 1727 was a golden one for the community whose hearts were again being knit together by the Holy Spirit, but God wasn't satisfied with a mere revival. In early August, Zinzendorf and fourteen other Moravian brethren spent a night in conversation and prayer. A short time later, on August 13, the community experienced "a day of the outpourings of the Holy Spirit upon the congregation; it was its Pentecost."[1] It was an experience that would change the world.

That is because the Moravians didn't only experience revival that summer, they made it a permanent part of their community's culture and governance. Before the end of that month, twenty-four men and twenty-four women pledged to pray one hour a day in turn for every hour of the day, seven days a week. This "hourly intercession" continued nonstop for the next one hundred years. (Now you should be able to grasp why this trip to Herrnhut marked my life so much!) One of the key passages that God gave them during that time is found in Leviticus 6:13:

A fire shall always be burning on the altar; it shall never go out.

As a result, the Moravians grew together to become a community like none the world had ever seen before. God was with Zinzendorf, and he was able to form the community into a semimonastic group based upon family life rather than the typical celibates. They lived and worked together in community as farmers and craftsmen. It was certainly a version of God's "city on a hill" from which His light would shine around the world.

A band of single brethren pledged together that they would pursue whatever God called them to do. In 1731, Lord Zinzendorf met a former African slave from the island of St. Thomas who had been converted to Christianity. He was at the Danish court while Zinzendorf was visiting and expressed his desire for missionaries to come to teach his people. Upon learning of this, the community at Herrnhut was quick to respond. A young potter, Leonard Dober, and David Nitschmann, a carpenter, answered the call. Eventually, the community felt that Leonard Dober was to go without Nitschmann and he took Tobias Leopold, who went with him on a temporary basis. While many credit William Carey with being the father of modern missions, the Moravians were among the first Protestants to leave Europe to take God's Word to different ethnic groups and who inspired Carey to do the same. Everything the Moravians did began with prayer, was bathed in prayer, and was carried out in prayer. It was said that the Moravians sang a hundred hymns when Leonard was sent out. The gospel is reformational, and nations bound in darkness—both individually and corporately—have been touched as a result of the missionary movement begun by the Moravians.

A HERITAGE OF PRAYER AND SERVICE

While in Herrnhut, I asked to see the cemetery called God's Acre where they brought the Moravian missionaries to their final rest after giving their lives in foreign nations. My friend James Goll had told me about it. As we stood on the hill just below the watch-tower, I knew I was there to be marked by God like those who had gone before me. I knew that at some point during our visit I would be deeply changed.

Our friend Christian Winter, whose ancestors were among the Moravians who had prayed during those hundred years, walked us around and explained the area to us. (This is poignant for me now, as Christian has gone on to be with the Lord. He and his family were called to keep the twenty-four-hour watch of the Lord going in Herrnhut.) He explained that the men were buried on one side of the cemetery and the women on the other.

As we walked down the rows of markers, I noticed the names of countries on them—Suriname, Trinidad, and others. We walked past the crypt of Zinzendorf himself, and I began to tear up. The presence of the Lord was so strong. We knew that this was holy ground.

Moving to another part of the cemetery, we again stopped and read the tombstones. "Who is buried here?" I asked Christian.

"The children of the missionaries who went to foreign fields," he answered. Then I noticed their markers had the names of countries also. Christian went on: "The people who went sent their children back to be educated at six years of age. Some who returned as a child never saw their parents again in this life. While a few became bitter, a number of them went back to the same countries where their parents had served." I was struck by this. I could feel the mark of God—a deep imprint of the purposes of God, the faithfulness of God, and the love of God—pressing into my soul.

One particular story that I'd heard was about a group of teenage boys who left on a boat as missionaries. Their parents were weeping, knowing they might never see their children again. The young men called back to their parents, "Mom and Dad, do not weep! We go for the Lamb and the cross!"

The cross and the Lamb. Yes, as I heard that story I knew that I had just received the strength I needed to continue with the message: Nations can be reformed through radical followers with revolutionary biblical principles to disciple nations. Those who had gone before me, and the story of their lives, reached out and marked my life that day forever.

Three strands wrapped around everything the Moravians did. James Goll writes about these in his book *The Lost Art of Intercession*:

1. They had relational unity, spiritual community, and sacrificial living.

2. The power of their persistent prayer produced a divine passion and zeal for missionary outreach to the lost. Many of them even sold themselves into slavery in places like Suriname in South America just so they could carry the light of the gospel into closed societies. The Moravians were the first missionaries to the slaves

of St. Thomas in the Virgin Islands; they went to strange places called Lapland and Greenland and to many places in Africa.

3. The third strand was described by a motto that they lived by: "No one works unless someone prays." They took the form of a corporate commitment to sustained prayer and ministry to the Lord. This prayer went on unbroken for twenty-four hours a day, seven days a week, every day of each year for over one hundred years.[2]

Point three bears closer examination, as there was a marriage of intercessory prayer and work that we need to learn from in our generation. It seems to be reemerging today in the 24/7 prayer movement. This type of intercession is so important that I am going to spend a whole chapter dealing with its importance in reforming nations.

ANOTHER PIECE OF THE PUZZLE

I didn't mention earlier, in my excitement to tell about our visit to Herrnhut, that our stop in Prague was also unplanned in the original journey. At that time, I was praying about writing this book, and my visit to Prague was part of the reformation trail that I didn't know about.

Prague is a magnificent city, but I didn't know much about its history until we were standing in a plaza looking up at the bronze statue of a man named John Huss. While reading the plaque, I realized that this was the man whose teachings had first inspired the Moravians and made him a martyr. My curiosity was piqued. Who was this reformer?

John Huss is known as the Reformer of Bohemia (the area that is now the Czech Republic). One of the "heretical" things he taught was that people should be able to read the Bible in their own language. Prior to his time, only the clergy were allowed to read the

Word, and it was in Latin. Huss had been greatly influenced by the writings of John Wycliffe, who also believed that the people should be able to read the Bible in their own language. It is hard for us today to imagine why this should be such a revolutionary thing.

Huss was an educated man and was appointed as rector at the university in Prague. During one period of his life, he encountered great favor both with the common people and the nobility. Leaders today will tell you that favor can be fleeting, so don't think too highly of yourself if you are at the top; the same people who love you one day might crucify you the next—just ask Jesus!

The more John Huss studied the Scripture, the more he came to realize how far the church had slipped away from sound biblical beliefs. One of the practices that he found most offensive was one that Martin Luther would speak out against a century later—that of selling forgiveness through indulgences. In other words, you could pay to be forgiven and cut down your time in purgatory. Not only that, but you could buy your friends and relatives safe passage to heaven as well, even if they had already died. Again, for most Christians today it is absolutely absurd to think that anyone could believe such a thing, but this is because we can read the Bible in our own language to find out the truth for ourselves!

Huss became more radical in his speaking and writing as time passed. His preaching in the Bethlehem Chapel was in Czech, the common language of the people, unlike the Latin liturgy they were used to. In 1403, his university prohibited a disputation he had written on forty-five theses taken in part from Wycliffe. The leadership and staff of the university soon labeled his writings heretical and asked that he return to accepted doctrine. However, the truth had already changed him, and he could not give in. In response to their requests, he wrote:

Even if I should stand before the stake which has been prepared for me, I would never accept the recommendation of the theological faculty.[3]

During this time, a general council in Rome condemned the writings of Wycliffe, the Bible translator, and ordered them burned. Two hundred of his manuscripts were seized and destroyed. In addition, all free preaching, such as that done by John Huss, was to stop, or those who did so would pay extreme consequences.

The fires of persecution heated up after this, and Huss fled into virtual exile. He continued his writings and proclaimed that the foundation of the church was Christ, not Peter. This was the same position that Augustine had taken in his *Retractions*.[4]

Persecution would turn into betrayal as a general council was called in Constance, Switzerland, and Huss was summoned to appear. The Holy Roman Emperor, Sigismund, promised him safe passage coming and going, and Huss believed him, although his friends warned him that it was a trap. Unfortunately, his friends turned out to be right and the emperor did not protect him, fearing that he would be held responsible for shielding a heretic. When Huss arrived in Constance, he was imprisoned for seventy-three days in chains. During this time, he was also denied contact with friends and was poorly fed. As a result of his age and the conditions of his cell, he fell dangerously ill and suffered a good deal because of it.

On June 5, 1415, he was brought to trial for the first time. All along John Huss asked only to be charged with crimes against the Scriptures and proclaimed he was willing to recant if they could prove to him that he had violated any of them. Instead, he was charged for his support and defense of Wycliffe's teachings, some of which he had never taught or addressed in any way.

In response to being condemned to die on July 6, 1415, he exclaimed:

> O God and Lord, now the council condemns even thine own act and thine own law as heresy, since thou thyself didst lay thy cause before thy Father as the just judge, as an example for us, whenever we are sorely oppressed.[5]

Six bishops stripped Huss of his clerical vestment and crammed a tall cap covered with pictures of the devil onto his head. They excommunicated him and committed his soul to the devil.

As he arrived at the Episcopal Palace, he saw a pile of wood and thought it was where he would be executed. Instead the wood was lit on fire, and his writings brought and thrown into the flames.

After they forced him to witness this, they proceeded on and stopped in a large area where they had piled wood and straw. Then they took a garment prepared with pitch and tar and put it on him.

Chains secured his neck and legs to the stake. More straw was piled up to his chin to make sure that he burned brightly in a hot fire. The straw was then kindled with John Wycliffe's own manuscript as Huss sang, "Christ, thou Son of the living God, have mercy upon me." With his last breath he prophesied, "You are now going to burn a goose (Huss means "goose" in Bohemian), but in a century you will have a swan which you can neither roast nor boil."[6] Roughly one hundred years later, in 1517, Martin Luther nailed his famous Ninety-Five Theses of Contention onto the church door at Wittenberg. The prophecy of John Huss had come to pass.

REFORMATIONAL LIVING

A third piece of this puzzle God put into place for me in my reformational thinking had happened a few years earlier when my husband,

Mike, and I were driving through the countryside of Pennsylvania. We were ministering in Allentown, and right next door is a city named Bethlehem. Near Bethlehem is a little town called Nazareth. We noted all the biblical names in the area, including the Jordan stream that runs through Allentown.

As we drove around, I suddenly remembered hearing from a friend that the Moravians had settled there from Herrnhut. *Could this be another piece of my journey?* I wondered. I excitedly asked my friend Marilyn if there was a Moravian museum of some sort around the region. "Oh yes," she replied in her perky way, "there's one in Bethlehem."

"Let's go!" I exclaimed. So Mike and I and our young friend Laura trekked off on an adventure to learn more about their settlement.

As we entered the museum I could hardly believe what I was seeing! Count Zinzendorf's Moravians had come here to establish a community to evangelize the Native Americans and minister to the African American slaves in the area. Tracing the history of their journey was fascinating. They first came to Nazareth (about four miles from Bethlehem) from Georgia in 1740, to settle at the invitation of George Whitefield, the great English evangelist. He wanted to build a home for the African American orphans.

During their trip over from England several years earlier, two young men, John and Charles Wesley, traveled on the same ship with their party. While on board, a great storm arose, and the Moravians showed no fear but gathered together to sing hymns and worship God. John Wesley, although a minister, was not yet born again. He was so impacted by their calmness in the face of possible death that he was inspired to learn more about this type of "heart faith." After John returned to England, another Moravian, Peter Bohler, would finally lead him to a personal revelation of Jesus Christ. It was after this "conversion experience" that John launched the series of great revivals in England that were a part of what came to be known as the Great Awakening. They also proved to be the beginnings of the Methodist movement.

According to the accounts in the museum, the Moravians were initially funded through Zinzendorf's patronage. They planned provisions for their people and fed them well before the trip to America so they would embark healthy enough to make the journey to the new land. Once they'd settled, they had an amazing marketplace anointing focused on supporting their missionary outreach.

It is fascinating how far Zinzendorf's influence reached during his lifetime. He himself was greatly impacted by his godfather, Philipp Jakob Spener, the father of the Pietist movement. The young count's father died just six weeks after he was born, and so his godfather had an important place in his life. Spener underwent persecution while on the theological faculty at Wittenberg and was discharged in 1695 for 264 errors. Only his death released him from the opposition he faced.

A generational anointing from this spiritual line was passed on to the young Zinzendorf, who was trained, like Martin Luther, as a lawyer and initially set upon a diplomatic career. Zinzendorf's pious grandmother, Catherine von Gersdorf, also helped shape his life and character. This blending and pouring from one generation to the other was very important. It is equally important today for the different generations to stay connected and continually learn from one another.

As a teenager, Zinzendorf formed a society called the Order of the Grain of Mustard Seed. This society deemed to use their influence as young nobles to extend the gospel. Later, as Zinzendorf grew to adulthood, he reactivated the society and recruited other influential members, such as the King of Denmark, the Archbishop of Canterbury, and the Archbishop of Paris. It is fascinating in light of the emphasis the Lord is putting on the marketplace and business to see how a young man of great wealth used his money and influence to change the world.

Once in Nazareth, the Moravians built dormitories for the thirty-two young married couples who had come over from Herrnhut. They also built a "Sisters House" for the single women and a "Brethren House" for the single men. In addition, they constructed a "Widows House" for the widows of Moravian missionaries. (I am not proposing we live like this today, although some might want to, but there are lessons to be gleaned from the way the Moravians lived in community together.) After beginning in Nazareth, they moved on to Bethlehem.

The Moravians were so innovative in building communities that various people came to see their enterprises. These included John Adams, then of the Continental Congress and later President of the United States. John wrote his wife Abigail about Bethlehem. From his letters we learn that they had a shared economic system based on communal living.

In these budding towns, everyone worked for the good of the community. Each was assigned a task to learn as a child and would be apprenticed in that profession. In this fashion, they each pursued their unique role in meeting their community's needs from clothing to health care to foundries. They also excelled in the making of musical instruments—not surprising for a group who loved to sing praises to their Lord. They were known as excellent craftsmen and their products were known for their quality. Initially, they received everything they needed to sustain life in place of wages. Around 1760, the same year that Count Zinzendorf passed away, this practice was abandoned in favor of receiving traditional wages.

As a musician, I was fascinated by the stories of their trombonists, who played music at the various important moments in the life of the community. For instance, if someone died, they would go to the top of the houses and play certain songs to inform everyone of the death.

They were also famous for their painters and songwriters. However, one of their most important contributions to modern-day society came with the development of a graded educational system for children. Another educational innovation, introduced by Comenius—a Moravian who was not in that community but influenced them—was illustrated picture books. Also important to the community was the language school for training new missionaries who would be sent to unreached people groups. Education is such an important part of reformation and renewing the minds of a nation that it cannot be stressed too much. These are keys to understanding the function of a Holy Nation.

The Moravians had a community with a purpose. They existed for something greater than themselves and their everyday subsistence and well-being. God had given them a passion to see Native Americans saved as well as African Americans. However, their mandate went far beyond salvation to societal reformation through education and community development. They formed one of the first truly integrated societies. Racism was unknown in their villages.

In fact, one of the stories I read was about a visit from emissaries of the Nanticokes and Shawnees, who said they also represented the Delaware and Mahicans, their brothers. In the story of a covenant made between them and the Moravians who had come as missionaries, the native leader continually addressed what he called "his brown and his white brothers" as one tribe.

The Moravians were Christians not only in word but also in deed. They would venture out to find the natives where they were starving and bring relief. Because of this, the native people saw the love of Christ and wanted Him as their Savior.

While the Moravians weren't perfect, and the societal structure they established didn't last, their accomplishments were landmarks in the history of God's kingdom. Even though they have been largely overlooked, their example and their culture have tremendous lessons for us today—especially if we are to become reformers of nations.

THE UNITY OF TRUTH

Although these stories are divided by centuries in a world where communication was much more difficult than it is today, it is interesting that they hold so much in common. For example, Luther spoke against many of the same things Huss did even when it is unlikely he was ever exposed to Huss' writings. Luther stood against indulgences and for a Bible translated into the common tongue so it could be understood by all. One of Luther's major accomplishments was the translation of the Bible into German. That, coupled with the earlier invention of the Gutenberg printing press, allowed copies of the Bible to be put into the hands of ordinary people. The Luther Bible contributed greatly to the convergence of the modern German language and is regarded as a landmark in German literature. The 1534 edition was also profoundly influential on William Tyndale's translation as well as the King James Bible.[7]

What literature did Huss, Luther, and Zinzendorf share in common that influenced them equally? More than anything else, it was the Holy Scriptures. These men came to unmovable faith in God and conviction of truth when they chose to look at the Bible as the basis of all things that pertain to life and godliness. It was the basis of the Reformation itself and is still the basis of individual, cultural, and national reformation today.

We need to realize that these men weren't great because of any special characteristics they had on their own. Luther was a man with feet of clay, and later in his life he became embittered at the Jews and wrote horrific things against them. While this is not to be excused, we can see that God also used Luther in great ways that are still touching us today. Why? Because when he lined up with God's Word, great and powerful transformation took place, and when he didn't, he fell into error like anyone else could. We need to get into the Word ourselves so that we can live according to it as much as the good examples of our past did.

As reformers, we must realize that we always stand upon the shoulders of those who have gone before us. Many of them paid a great price as groundbreakers in the truth so that we might have the liberty to live by the written Word today. This is why the generations must stay connected not only in relationship but also in knowledge. We need to know the path others have walked so we can build upon the foundation they have laid and not repeat their mistakes.

My mentor, Peter Wagner, has paid a heavy price for being willing to release the new things that God is revealing to His people through the Scriptures. One day I was looking at a magazine and discovered that in the first half the writers were taking him to task for his writings on church growth, and in the second half they were criticizing his teachings about spiritual warfare. He once told me he just laughs at these things and checks to see if they have spelled his name right! While he is very interested in being biblically correct, he is not afraid of risk-taking or standing up for the unpopular things God has shown him in the Word.

I had heard him talking about what he calls the "diffusion of innovation" during a message one day and phoned to ask him more about it. "Oh," he said, "I wrote about that in my book *Confronting the Powers*" (one of his earlier books on the subject of prayer and spiritual warfare). Later that day he sent me the reference. This is what he had to say about the process that happens around deformational truth:

> Social scientists propound what they call "diffusion of innovation theory" in which they explain that whenever new ideas are introduced into social networks, a predictable process is set into motion. Four kinds of sequential responses usually follow the initiatives of the innovators. They are called (1) early adopters, (2) middle adopters, (3) late adopters, and (4) nonadopters. This happens in the Christian community as well as in society in general. Few today recall that when the Sunday school movement was proposed by an innovator, Robert Raikes, strong criticism was directed against him from many directions. I mention that because we now live in a generation in which it would be extremely rare to find a Christian leader opposed to the Sunday school on principle. The most intense controversy takes place during the period of the early adopters, which is exactly where the ideas revolving around strategic-level spiritual warfare find themselves today.[8]

Peter Wagner went through a number of paradigm shifts during his many years of ordained ministry. One only has to read the seventy-plus books he has written to know that. He goes on in *Confronting the Powers* to relate about a time when he teamed with John Wimber during the power evangelism movement:

In the 1980s John Wimber and I took a great deal of flak about power evangelism and our teachings on divine healing, miracles and casting out demons. Strong voices that still object to these on principle are now few and far between.[9]

While I have not gone through the firestorms anywhere near what Peter Wagner has, I can look back and remember the early-adopter stage for such topics as spiritual warfare, prophecy, and women in ministry, to name a few. Most of these movements are in the mid-to-late-adopter stage now. Of course, there are still some who are non-adopters and teach against those practices and doctrines.

Gilbert Bilezikian stresses an important point that all must learn to be a reformer when he says:

> Every generation of Christians needs to examine its beliefs and practices under the microscope of Scripture to identify and purge away those worldly accretions that easily beset us, and to protect jealously the freedom dearly acquired for us—both men and women—on the hill of Calvary.[10]

Today, just as in the times of Huss, Luther, and the Moravians, God is calling for believers of all generations to rise up, listen to the Holy Spirit together, and make adjustments to our religious structures without fear of persecution. There is too often a desire to resist something new God is doing for the sake of traditions that are not found anywhere in the Bible. Others want to keep their control and positions of power in a church body rather than letting God have His way. They choose to give in to religious spirits and legalism rather than let God touch lives and transform their communities. Such religious spirits are mean and sometimes deadly, but this should never stop us from following the Way, the Truth, and the Life.

This reminds me of a conversation I had one day with my preacher daddy, Albert S. Johnson. "Daddy," I quizzed, "what should I do if I find out the way we have believed on different issues isn't right?" My dad smiled that special kind of smile that made me feel like I was the most important person in the world and said, "Sweetheart, never be afraid to search for the truth. If you have it, you won't lose it." That was really good advice. It has given me the confidence to be an early adopter in several new moves of God without fear.

Fear cripples innovators. While we all may deal with it at times, as those called to be world changers we can't let it stop us. We have to be willing always to speak the truth in love and stand up for the biblical convictions God has put into our hearts.

We follow in some big steps as we look back at the generations of reformers who have gone before us. Each of us will leave some kind of legacy to those who come after us as well. I want mine to be a good one, and I know you want yours to be as well.

Chapter Three

DISCIPLING NATIONS

IMAGINE A WORLD where you turn on the television set and you don't have to screen what your children watch. Violent crime is unusual. The Internet doesn't need to be filtered for content. What about mega-cities where people ask, "What is the bad part of town?" and you reply, "My city doesn't have such a section. None of it is bad." Think about the possibility of grandparents walking their dog after dark in the inner city with no fear of being mugged. Imagine government social services and welfare offices closing down because those needs are being met by the local churches and faith-based nonprofits. Gang violence, homelessness, drug pushers, and drive-by shootings are all things of the past.

"Utopia?" you say. "No," I would answer, "what I am describing is a nation discipled and taught of the Lord."

Did your heart leap within you as you read that first paragraph? Did a longing for it begin to grow? My heart yearns to see all of this come to pass in my city. Yet is this really possible, or do we have to wait until Christ's return? I am not saying that there will not be any more evil or sin in the world. However, just as there are areas of the world that are very safe, with little or no crime, I do believe that with the power of God, we can disciple our cities until this becomes the norm for us as well. Just look at how church-going communities differ from those where God is not known or valued.

How can we tip the balance in God's favor? Is it even possible? Let's consider some Scriptures together and see what you think for yourself. The concept of discipling nations that I wrote about in Chapter One doesn't begin with the last words of Christ on the earth in the Great Commission. It all began in the garden.

GOD'S ORIGINAL PLAN

The garden of Eden was a beautiful place, full of order, running according to God's design. God's law was universally obeyed. Adam and Eve, the first couple, were created in God's image with a purpose and given an earthly mandate:

> *Be fruitful and multiply; fill the earth and subdue it; have dominion over the fish of the sea, over the birds of the air, and over every living thing that moves on the earth* (Genesis 1:28).

Do we still have that same purpose and mandate today as human beings created in the image of God? This dominion passage has never been rescinded, so our answer should be yes. It didn't change with the fall. It simply makes sense that God's original purpose for humanity on the earth has never changed.

Being created in the image of God has a broad, sweeping scope that is governmental in nature. That government consists of a King and His appointed regents over His kingdom on the earth. *Nelson's New King James Version Study Bible* gives this insight into our being made in the image of God:

> In ancient times an emperor might command statues of himself to be placed in remote parts of his empire. These

symbols would declare that these areas were under his power and reign. So God placed humankind as living symbols of Himself on earth to represent His reign. We are made to reflect His majesty on the earth, have dominion: Rule as God's regent.[1]

As I read those words I pondered to myself, "Why haven't we fulfilled that purpose?" Looking around the earth today one can certainly tell that we haven't even begun to fill, subdue, and have dominion over the earth in any positive way. Hebrews 2:5-9 acknowledges this. Instead we see poverty, violence, disease, homelessness, hunger, endless wars, and other major problems.

Our Genesis mandate to fill, subdue, and have dominion over the earth reminds us that God loves us, His children, but He also loves the world. He wants the world to be saved. He says so in John 3:16: *"For God so loved the world that He gave His only begotten Son."* God so loved the world or *kosmos*. *Thayer's Greek Lexicon* says this means "an apt or harmonious arrangement or constitution order." We tend to interpret this Scripture as referring only to our salvation from hell. While it does refer to that, salvation means a great deal more than escape from judgment. It also means that God loves His creation—the earth itself. Otherwise, why didn't John say, "For God so loved humankind that He gave His only begotten Son"?

We need to realize that Jesus' main emphasis was not the gospel of salvation but the gospel of the kingdom of God. Jesus' first teaching was not "Repent so that you can be saved" or even "God loves you and has a wonderful plan for your life," but *"Repent, for the kingdom of heaven is at hand"* (Matt. 4:17). Jesus wasn't looking for converts to a new religion; He was inviting people into a new kingdom, with a new government and a new King. He was inviting people to live heaven on earth. Look again at His first recorded sermon and all the reasons why He came:

> *The Spirit of the Lord is upon Me, because He has anointed Me to preach the gospel to the poor; He has sent Me to heal the brokenhearted, to proclaim liberty to the captives and recovery of sight to the blind, to set at liberty those who are oppressed; to proclaim the acceptable year of the Lord. ...Today this Scripture is fulfilled in your hearing* (Luke 4:18-19,21).

In Jesus' own words, He said His kingdom would address the poor, the mentally and emotionally ill, the physically sick, the blind, and those who sought justice. Jesus wasn't only creating the church; He was describing the new government of the kingdom of heaven.

Jesus wasn't looking to get people to change so much as He was looking to get kingdoms to change. He wanted to deliver God's people, and anyone else who would accept Him as Lord and Savior, out of the kingdom of darkness and into the kingdom of light. He wanted to replace man's justice—political, social, and religious—with God's justice. He wasn't looking to overthrow the power of Caesar but to usher all of the Roman Empire into the kingdom of God.

God created the world—loves it still in all its creation—and has put us here on the earth to be its stewards. We are His regents and ambassadors on the earth. In other words, God so loved the world that He wanted not only us as individuals to be saved in every sense of the word but the systems of the world He created to be redeemed as well—to be bought back and brought back—to His initial plans for them. This includes the environment. We are still stewards of the earth as well as all living things in it.

LIVING IN THE KINGDOM OF GOD[2]

One of the new movements we are seeing develop in nation after nation today is in the marketplace or workplace. God is calling men and women to run their businesses according to biblical principles. Following this example, leaders in law, government, real estate, the sciences, and other institutions of society are also hearing God's call to return to His precepts in each of their fields.

One of the key concepts of the Reformation was *coram Deo*—all of life is lived "before the face of God." In other words, there was no separation between the sacred and the secular—you didn't do things Monday through Saturday that you needed to repent of on Sunday. Instead, you lived all of life as though it were church all the time; only the means of worship changed day to day. On Sunday you might praise God with singing and listening to the Word, and on Thursday it would be in the way you performed your daily duties in the workplace and how you treated the people you interacted with.

The Holy Spirit brings to light the subjects of discipling, teaching, and stewarding the world through two groundbreaking, paradigm-shattering passages of Scripture. The first takes place when Jesus is in a mentoring session with His disciples, teaching them about prayer. We call this the Lord's Prayer, though it would be more accurate to call it the Disciple's Prayer.

My journey into being a reformer and discipler of nations actually began with my study on prayer. My first book, *Possessing the Gates of the Enemy*, is about intercession. I have been a student of prayers in the Bible throughout my ministry. At the time I wrote *Possessing*, I didn't fully understand how intercession and God's command that we have dominion on the earth tied together in this prayer. Note that the prayer is corporate in nature, not personal.

Our Father in heaven, hallowed be Your name. Your kingdom come. Your will be done on earth as it is in heaven. Give us this day our daily bread. And forgive us our debts, as we forgive our debtors. And do not lead us into temptation, but deliver us from the evil one. For Yours is the kingdom and the power and the glory forever. Amen (Matthew 6:9-13).

As I studied this powerful prayer the thought came to me: *Do I really believe that I should pray for the will of God to be done on the earth?* My next thought was: *What is God's will on earth now?*

I know there is a future kingdom, but the Bible also speaks of the present kingdom of God. What is possible here on earth today? What does the present kingdom of God look like? Little did I realize that I was going through a radical, reformational shift in understanding my role on the earth as a believer in Christ.

After studying Matthew 6:9-13, I realized that this was an intercessory prayer for one who is called not only to make disciples of individuals but of nations. If we are to pray for God's kingdom to come and His will to be done, then it is imperative that we also learn how to do the will of God.

As I read this prayer, I suddenly thought, *If part of this prayer is for the here and now—that we are to work to see God be Lord over not only our family affairs but our cities and nations—then the rest of the prayer must be understood in that same vein. It is not only for the individual; it is also a prayer of intercession for the nations.*

With that thought in mind, I began to study each part of the prayer.

"Our Father in heaven, hallowed be Your name." *Hallowed* according to *Thayer's Bible Dictionary* means "to render or declare holy, consecrate, or to separate from things profane and dedicate to God." We could paraphrase this by saying, "Father, holy is Your name." Because this is true, the inference biblically is "God, let Your name be holy and revered in every aspect of our kingdom life. Holy be Your name in my neighborhood, my city, and my society."

"Give us this day our daily bread" has the broader meaning of petitioning God to give us a plan to feed the poor on a large scale and deal with systemic poverty around the world. It is holy and righteous to do these things, and God will help us to do them if we ask for His wisdom in how to do it.

Asking forgiveness for our own debts could include following God's economic plan to deliver people from poverty and the backbreaking bondage of always owing money to others. The borrower is, after all, servant to the lender (see Prov. 22:7).

In fact, these premises are so broad in scope that I am going to take whole chapters and explore them as we delve into our role as believers on the earth as it relates to justice, government, economics, education, and other kingdom of heaven issues addressed in this prayer.

WHAT IS GOD'S WILL FOR THE EARTH?

If we are going to pray, "God's will be done," doesn't it make sense to look at what God's will is as expressed in the Bible? He made one part of His will clear in His last command to His disciples: "Go— disciple and teach nations" (see Matt. 28:19-20). We could rephrase the command to disciple nations in this manner: *"Go and release the Jesus in you into every nation."*

One could simply ask, "What would Jesus do and say about the problems we face in the world today?" However—if you would indulge me—let me give you a heavy-duty version of the same question: "How do we see the incarnated Savior manifested through us in society?"

Here are some synonyms for *incarnation*: integration, inclusion, incorporation, manifestation, and systemization. In other words, how do we see the kingdom of God come into every aspect of society? What would it look like if God's wisdom and righteousness were incorporated into our laws, government, educational systems, as well as into our workplaces, homes, and everything we do?

If God's Word is systemic in how it applies to our needs for biblical justice—how we feed the poor and take care of single mothers, for example—letting it direct us in how we deal with each of these areas releases the incarnation of that Word, Jesus Christ, into every situation.[2]

Social justice is not necessarily the same as biblical justice. Social justice may change as a society moves away from following God's Word. Biblical justice never changes in its principles in areas such as abortion and human trafficking and slavery.

Nations will be discipled when the incarnation of Christ is manifested at every level of society. To put it more simply, God wants His Word and presence felt in everything we think, plan, and do. Then everything is done "before the face of God" the way He has instructed us to do it. We are to be part of seeing His kingdom manifest now while still understanding that there is a greater future kingdom to come one day when Jesus returns.

After I had the revelation that the kingdom of God was important in my time and that I had a role in seeing it implemented, I started studying my Bible with new excitement every day, trying to better understand God's kingdom principles. One very important verse came alive for me:

> *And this **gospel of the kingdom** will be preached in all the world as a witness to all the nations, and then the end will come* (Matthew 24:14).

"This gospel of the kingdom will be preached" echoed in my spirit as I read this. For my whole adult life, I had thought that we would preach the gospel of salvation to all the world, and when everyone had heard, Jesus would return, but this is not what Scripture says. It says we should be preaching the good news of the kingdom of heaven. In other words, it is not so much about answered altar calls as it is about inducting people into a new government—God's kingdom on earth. This gives me a much bigger responsibility for the world than I had previously understood.

Combining these two biblical passages together—Matthew 24:14 with the Disciple's Prayer in Matthew 6:9-13—challenges us toward whole new levels as believers. And when you add Matthew 28:18-20—the Great Commission that commands us to disciple nations—into the mix, you can't help but experience an incredible paradigm shift. For me, it completely redefined how I saw my role as a believer on the earth. We are not only to create converts; we are to manifest God's will on earth "as it is in heaven."

This led me to a new series of questions: "If this is true, then how do we preach the gospel of the kingdom? What does it really mean to disciple or teach the nations of the earth? If we are called to disciple the world—and to love it as God loves it—how do we do that on a practical level?"

In the past I believed that when the gospel of salvation was preached in my city, it would change the fabric of society as well. I believed there is a correlation between the number of believers in a city and the godliness of government and culture in that city. For example, in a city with a large number of believers, poverty and corruption should be the exception and not the rule.

But as God was teaching me this, I began to wonder about my own city. I live in the Dallas/Fort Worth metroplex area of Texas.

I know for a fact that Dallas/Fort Worth has a reputation as a densely Christian city. So does Colorado Springs, where our ministry was located before we moved back to our home area in Dallas. However, both areas have poor sections, and their city governments struggle with the same moral issues as most other U.S. cities of their size. Though largely Christian, these areas are still not discipled and taught of the Lord.

Why is this? What is wrong?

It would seem that the number of Christians who live in an area should change the spiritual climate of that area, but I didn't have to look far before I saw that simply wasn't the case. Why is that? I think the answer lies in two main areas: 1) perhaps we as believers have not seen kingdom living and building as our role; or 2) if we have, we don't know how to practically use biblical principles to change our cities into places where the will of God flows freely.

CREATING HOLY CITIES IN HOLY NATIONS

Imagine again for a moment what a place would look like where God's will freely reigned. A place where spiritual darkness is so weakened or defeated by the presence of light in the children of God that answers to prayer are unhindered, and God's blessings are available like fruit on trees that only needs to be harvested and distributed. A place where the body of Christ is alive and vibrant and healing flows to all that the body touches physically, emotionally, mentally, and spiritually. Certainly all would still have a right to freedom of religion, but people would know of Christians in every square foot of the city and respect them for their wisdom, conscientiousness, and loving-kindness toward others.

But this isn't happening because we as Christians are more influenced by our culture than we are by our Bibles. In the United States, we have accepted, for example, the separation of church and state as a good thing because of the corrupt church-run states of the past. However, the most horrific crimes of all time have not been perpetrated by church-run states. Even now in the U.S. we are allowing atheists to have the loudest voice in dictating how we express religion in public places. Though we live in a democracy, we are allowing a minority to control the majority. Many Christians have dismissed being politically involved, and our nation has suffered for it. We look to man's wisdom instead of God's for answers, and we are reaping a harvest of godlessness.

What we need is a radical shift in our worldview. We need to again see it as our responsibility to disciple nations and be radical reformers in our own nation. A key biblical building block in this process of shifting from a secular culture to a kingdom-of-heaven paradigm is found in both the New and the Old Testaments:

> *You are a chosen people, a royal priesthood, a holy nation, God's special possession, that you may declare the praises of him who called you out of darkness into his wonderful light. Once you were not a people, but now you are the people of God.... Dear friends, I urge you, as foreigners and exiles.... Live such good lives among the pagans that, though they accuse you of doing wrong, they may see your good deeds and glorify God on the day he visits us* (1 Peter 2:9-12 NIV).

> *Now therefore, if you will indeed obey My voice and keep My covenant, then you shall be a special treasure to Me above all people; for all the earth is Mine. And you shall be to Me a kingdom of priests and a holy nation* (Exodus 19:5-6).

Who was this last passage written to? A bunch of former slaves. Not only had they been slaves, but their parents and parents' parents also had been slaves. The people of God had been slaves for four hundred years. Did they know how to make laws, govern themselves, or even think for themselves? Of course not. They were slaves. Every day of their lives their actions were decided by others. Yet God didn't call them to a new religion—He called them to become a new nation and establish a new kingdom.

This is why God began to give them the "how tos" concerning becoming a Holy Nation after the Exodus. This included the structure for government, legislative systems, judicial systems, as well as educational and economic systems. For instance, Deuteronomy 1:9-15 and Exodus 18 talk about a representative government where leaders were chosen from each tribe and set over groups of one thousand, one hundred, fifty, and ten. If the people of God followed the structure He gave them, it would result in transforming a nation of slaves into one of the wealthiest and most prosperous peoples on earth.

What does this mean for us today? Romans 11:16-24 tells us that we are the children of Abraham, grafted into the vine, with the full benefit package given to the children of Abraham. All of these points revolve around the fact that God called the sons of Abraham to be a Holy Nation—a call we as Christians have as the children of Abraham as well. How do we, in a practical way, function as a Holy Nation across the face of the earth today? I will pose some exciting possibilities in answer to that question in the pages and chapters to follow.

Becoming a Holy Nation may seem like a big stretch for us given the fact that some of us have trouble even working together as a church and that religious government has such a bad track record. I mean, we are still trying to get over the damage done during the

Crusades! After all of this you might ask, "How could we possibly work together as a Holy Nation to see His kingdom come and His will be done?"

I know that some of you are reeling as you are reading this and might be thinking, "Cindy, are you advocating an authoritarian take-over by Christians?"

No, of course not. I am not saying that we should use physical force to disciple nations but rather that we should establish ourselves through a spiritual revolution. Righteous reformers must take seriously their role in discipling nations from a Holy Nation worldview.

The biblical mandate to disciple nations is one that many leaders are working to understand. It is a concept that can help them manifest God's kingdom in their nations. In fact, God has given the desire to transform nations to many in leadership around the world—and, believe it or not, it is making a difference.

Examples of Biblical Transformation

There are some powerful examples of reformers in the Bible. One was a young king named Josiah. I love his story. He came to the throne when he was only eight years old. The Bible sums up his life in this way: *"He did what was right in the sight of the Lord"* (2 Kings 22:2).

One of the reasons I am so drawn to Josiah's story is that I know there are young government leaders, educators, scientists, doctors, and lawyers who are preparing to reform their societies and disciple their nations. Just like God chose Josiah, He is choosing the leaders of tomorrow by His Spirit today.

To put this story into a modern-day context, I am going to paraphrase it for you: When King Josiah was twenty-six years old, God began to speak to him about repairing the temple. He told him to find out how much money he had to do the work. The king asked two of his trusted subjects to go check out what funds had been collected in the temple offerings to start the remodeling. "Take the money," he commanded, as kings do, "and give it to the construction workers for repairs."

When his loyal leaders went to the temple, the senior pastor (high priest) said to Shaphan (one of the king's leaders), "I have found the Book of the Law in the house of the Lord!"[3]

Shaphan, whose job was to transcribe important documents and read them (perhaps like lawyers or congressional aides would today), took the book and read it out loud to King Josiah.

The king was beside himself with sorrow and grief when he realized how far his nation had fallen away from God! He tore his clothes as was the custom of the day when people were in mourning. He mourned and was in grief because he was the king of a nation that had not only strayed from following God's law but was in great danger of the Lord judging them for their sins.

What did this young king do to change the course of his nation? First, he repented before God, and then he looked around at his nation through God's eyes. All of a sudden he saw things that he hadn't noticed before—primarily that his nation was full of sin and idolatry. From that day forward he went about making changes to his nation as dictated in the Book of the Law, which had been lost in the temple but now was found.

From the reforms of Josiah, it is evident that this book contained much of the contents of the book of Deuteronomy[4]—the same book that the children of Israel were given to teach them how to become a Holy Nation.

One of my purposes in telling Josiah's story is to inspire you to study God's Word with new, reformational eyes. It is important not only to read God's Word but to interpret God's world in the light of His Word. We can reconcile and redeem nations through applying biblical principles today just like Josiah did in his time. In doing so we will be disciplers of nations—each doing our part in teaching nations to observe all God has commanded in the Book.

The Bible is our manufacturer's handbook. In it, God gives specific instructions on how the world best operates. It belongs to Him as Creator. He knows how to make it work.

To say to the Creator, "I can run this world the way I want to, do what I want with it, enact laws in the society about morality the way I want, and do anything that I want with my private life as long as I don't hurt anyone else" is totally ridiculous! Many things done "in private" hurt others. The "secret sins" of pornography and adultery are tearing our families apart, and the sins that societies allow within their midst build up until the very ground cries out to God just as Abel's blood did after Cain slew him.

That thinking could be likened to a person who has never owned a cell phone and doesn't read the instruction manual on how to use it. Instead, the person decides, "I don't need to turn the phone on the way the manual says, I want to start it the way I want to!" It simply won't work that way!

We have to do what the instruction book says in order to make it work.

In the same way, we can't enact laws that condone immorality simply because it is done in "private," or any other action that breaks God's rules. When you break God's law, creation breaks down—and societies do too.

During the years that Mike and I have had the ministry Generals International (originally founded as Generals of Intercession), we have worked in many nations that are in the process of transformation. Some of the brightest lights in the earth have lost their place of transformation.

One example is Almolonga, Guatemala. Almolonga was a disaster area at one time. Alcoholism was rampant, and it was a center of idolatry. The indigenous people of the village were in despair. Few had more than a sixth-grade education. Then a few brave souls got hold of God's Word and took on the process of the spiritual transformation of the area.

One of the miraculous signs that the city was changing was in the land itself. Once dry and unyielding, it became fertile and started to produce giant vegetables. I have been there myself, and all I have to say is whenever tourists want to get their pictures taken holding the broccoli, cauliflower, and carrots, you know they are huge!

The villagers started selling their vegetables all across Central America and became wealthy enough to afford to buy—for cash—Mercedes trucks to haul their produce! The jail shut down and became a restaurant. The idol worship center closed down because of a lack of participants. Ninety-five percent of the population is now born again!

As you drive through Almolonga today, you see street signs with names like "Glory to God." Mike and I know some of the leaders of that movement, and they are genuine and wonderful believers. What is happening in Almolonga gives us great hope for what can take place elsewhere if we would just apply prayerfully the principles of God's Word as the foundation for our societies.

HEALING NATIONS

The concept of societal transformation can be linked with another biblical ideal—the healing of nations. In order for a nation to be transformed, it needs to be reformed—what is corrupt in it needs to be amended and returned to what is true and righteous. When nations are reformed, they are also healed.

God first revealed to me that nations needed to be healed during a time of intercessory prayer for the United States in 1985. As I interceded for my nation, I asked the Lord the question, "Lord, since Satan is neither omniscient nor omnipresent, how has he made such inroads into the United States of America?" The Lord impressed upon me that Satan has a strategy for nations while God's people did not. He then went on with instructions to "gather the generals" to intercede for the nations that they might repent of their sin.

What is the sin of my nation? I wondered. I am embarrassed to say that I had not heard anyone preach about the specific sins of America at that time. Now, more than twenty years later, this is a common theme in the body of Christ. Second Chronicles 7:14 gives the biblical formula: Repent for the sins of your nation, and God will heal your land. When God first led me to teach on this subject, I had never heard anyone propose that a nation could be healed.

During that same time, the Lord elaborated this to me by telling me that we needed to repent for such things as the Trail of Tears, slavery, racism, and other historic sins of the United States. At the time, we also began to gather leaders to repent of the sins the various races had committed against other races. Many of these stemmed from perversions of the biblical understanding of all people being created in God's image, such as racism, slavery, unjust Jim Crow laws, ethnocentrism, Manifest Destiny, broken treaties, massacres, forced relocations and death marches, de facto segregation and discrimination, public lynchings, prevention of minorities from voting, unequal education, unequal opportunities, and violations of civil rights.

Time and again I have seen white leaders kneel in repentance and weep before their African American brothers and sisters. The sins of mistrust, theft, and imprisonment in internment camps against the Japanese Americans during World War II by the United States government were similarly dealt with, as were those sins against the host people of the land, the Native Americans. In our history, at least three hundred fifty treaties with Native American tribes have been broken by the U.S. government.

Several years ago Mike and I had the privilege of sitting in a government office while an official humbly repented for breaking these treaties. The Native American leaders had brought a volume listing all the treaties made with various tribes, and every one had been broken. The government leader held the thick book in his hands and with deep emotion prayed, "Father, I ask You to forgive the government that I represent for our sin against the host people of the land, the Native American people. I am so sorry for our sin." He then looked at the Native leaders and asked for their forgiveness as well.

This is a beautiful picture that is part of the fulfillment of Revelation 22:2:

> *In the middle of its street, and on either side of the river, was the tree of life, which bore twelve fruits, each tree yielding its fruit every month. The leaves of the tree were for the healing of the nations.*

As we become healed nations or peoples in our earthly identities, it will become increasingly easy for us to function as one. Just as it was for those at Herrnhut, unity is a key to our transformation and reformation today.

For the past twenty years our ministry has been working to see this kind of healing happen in all the nations to which we have traveled. However, there is still quite a bit of work to be done in this area. Racism, prejudice, and dishonest dealings between nations remain in the world, and this kind of repentance and reconciliation will need to continue. We'll never be able to say we're completely finished with this process, because each generation will need to acknowledge its unique dirty history. If each generation doesn't do this, it can convince itself that its ancestors were pure and not responsible for atrocities in the past, and that it was on the wronged side and therefore needs to take vengeance into its own hands. A false belief in a myth of purity is dangerous to anyone who happens to be outside their group. However, the major paradigm shift that I see in this new move of God is adding the dimension of reconciling all things to the list of reconciling all races.

The book of Acts tells us:

> *Repent therefore and be converted, that your sins may be blotted out, so that times of refreshing may come from the presence of the Lord, and that He may send Jesus Christ, who was preached to you before, whom heaven must receive until the times of restoration of all things* (Acts 3:19-21).

What does this passage mean by "all things"? My husband, Mike, teaches this "all things" restoration from Paul's letter to the Colossians:

> *For it pleased the Father that in Him all the fullness should dwell, and by Him to reconcile all things to Himself, by Him, whether things on earth or things in heaven, having made peace through the blood of His cross* (Colossians 1:19-20).

Mike points out that the Scripture doesn't say "all people" but "all things." "All things" means "all things." "All things" means "all structures, all parts of society, all groups of people." In fact, we have the ministry of reconciliation on earth given to us as an assignment by God to reconcile all things.

Therefore, if anyone is in Christ, he is a new creation; old things have passed away; behold, all things have become new. Now all things are of God, who has reconciled us to Himself through Jesus Christ, and has given us the ministry of reconciliation, that is, that God was in Christ reconciling the world to Himself, not imputing their trespasses to them, and has committed to us the word of reconciliation (2 Corinthians 5:17-19).

What do you think has been the major deterrent to our transforming or discipling our nations? I have a theory that it has been our understanding of where we should expend our time and energy in this season before the Lord's return.

Remember that we were commanded by the Lord to "do business till I come" in the parable of the minas (see Luke 19:12-27). The King James Version says, "Occupy till I come." It may be that our focus has been so much on the Lord's return that we missed the "occupy" part of our instruction. Part of our occupying is to do evangelism—to bring people to Christ and nurture them until Christ is fully formed in them. Another part is to fulfill the Genesis mandate to be fruitful, subdue, and have dominion over the earth (see Gen. 1:28). We are stewards of God's earth in every sense. Yet how do we "occupy" the business world, legal and legislative systems, government agencies and public services, educational institutions, and other sectors of society crucial to letting God's "goodwill toward men" reign in our nations? (See Luke 2:14.)

Now that you are with me in understanding the importance of this new kingdom thinking, it is time to look at each of these areas individually in the following chapters. Let's continue this journey together.

Chapter Four

THE JUST CAUSE

AS ONE GAZES back across the history of Christianity, it seems that our thinking has gone something like this: "If we simply had a sweeping revival, then our nations would become righteous on every level." Sad to say, while a revival of hearts is important, there also needs to be a societal reformation in order to maintain the nation as righteous. Revival can lead to transformation, but only reformation institutes sustainable change. There is a fight to join in addition to revival, one Christians have too often neglected.

Darrow L. Miller, in his insightful book *Discipling Nations*, says this:

> We normally think of war in physical terms: bombs, guns, troops, death, bodies. But viewing war as a clash not just of armies but also of ideas allows us to better see what is going on around us.
>
> ...Christianity has revealed that for the time being, there is a war going on between life and death, good and evil, God and Satan. This spiritual conflict is not just something we read about in our Bibles. It intrudes into our

everyday world of ideas and ideals, shaping our history, determining our future, and to a large extent controlling how we live.[1]

Why Isn't Revival Enough?

One day Mike and I were dialoguing with a group of Christian leaders at a conference we were attending on the subject of transformation when I asked, "How do we maintain the change that comes with revival? How do we know that the societies we have seen transformed will still be living for God in a decade, let alone a hundred years from now?"

If you study the subject, you'll find that some revivals have had dramatic, long-reaching consequences. Luther's Reformation led to Protestantism, and Protestantism led to many social experiments, including the American experiment and opening of the door to new ways of thinking about government, science, economics, politics, education, the relation of church and state, and so on.

We've also had several significant revival periods in American history, including the First Great Awakening with Gilbert Tennet, Jonathan Edwards, and George Whitefield from 1740 to 1742; the Second Great Awakening beginning in the early 1800s with revivalist camp meetings; a national revival in 1831 spurred by Charles Finney's preaching and revival in Rochester, New York; a Civil War revival among Southern army troops; a post-Civil War Third Great Awakening with Dwight L. Moody and John Mott, who was a long-time president of the YMCA and helped found the Student Volunteer Movement, which lasted all the way until World War I; and a Fourth Great Awakening that began near the turn of the twentieth century with the Azusa Street Revival, and that has led to four hundred million Pentecostal/Charismatics in the worldwide movement after a mere one hundred years. Since World War II, America has experienced several streams of awakening that included the latter rain/healing movement, the prophetic movement, Billy Graham evangelistic meetings, and the ministries of InterVarsity, Navigators, Campus Crusade, Campus Life, Young Life, and others. All of these movements have contributed to what our society is about. But all revivals include two dynamics: they bring about both spiritual awakening and spiritual opposition. The devil plays on human gullibility and weakness to subvert revivals even as they begin.

Most revivals have proven to last only a few years. The Welsh Revival, for instance, went from approximately 1904 to 1906, depending on which account one reads. It is said that around one hundred thousand were born again during that time. The fire of God swept the nation and revival brought radical transformation. Things changed so much, in fact, that the donkeys that worked the coal mines had to be retrained because they were so used to receiving curses as commands. When the workers didn't curse anymore, the donkeys didn't know what to do. Bars closed because people stopped having the "demon drink." Prayer meetings were more popular than rugby matches—now that is amazing! It was a singing revival, as praises to God rang forth from the nation.

Yet even with most of the nation saved, Wales fell backward, influenced by anti-God philosophies such as Darwinism and an educational system aimed at making students employable rather than teaching them how to live. (I will go into these influences in the coming chapters.) Some say it was a lack of maturity and of sound biblical teaching, as the leader of the movement, Evan Roberts, was only twenty-six and went into seclusion only months after the revival began.

I don't think age matters, however. King Josiah was also twenty-six at the time he led national reform, and that reform stuck. Perhaps the failure of the revival to have staying power in Wales was the result of a lack of spiritual fathers mature enough to disciple the people into staying solid in their faith and teaching them how to make that faith the basis of their government and culture. Rees Howells, a prominent leader who emerged from the ranks of the coal miners during the Welsh Revival, emphasized the need for a prayer movement to sustain revival, and I concur. In fact, I will dedicate a chapter later in this book to "legislating in the heavens," which must be done in order to see a nation discipled.

What is the solution, then? I propose that a massive paradigm shift back to a biblical worldview is needed on every level. To reform, again, means "to amend what is corrupt; to return things to their God-ordained order and organization." Many today are talking about the transformation of their nations, but transforming a nation is really only "changing the outward form or appearance." Without a reformation, we will never see lasting transformation.

Our Need to Renew Our Minds

Ironically, most of us do not even know that our thinking and worldview have been polluted, or at least influenced, by secularism, naturalism, and humanistic rationalism through our educational system, media, and culture. We do not have a clue as to where to start in the process of reforming our nations. First, we don't see things the way God sees them. Even when we come to Scripture, we too often interpret it through culture-tinted glasses rather than digging into God's Word and letting it reform our hearts and renew our thinking. To be frank, Christianity today is simply lacking in Christ—God's Living Word revealed to us by the Holy Spirit through Bible study and prayer.

It isn't that the Bible is difficult to understand; it is that we don't bring the right questions to it. We spend a lot of time studying about prayer, the fruit of the Spirit, end-time events, and Christian character, but how often do we study the Bible for answers about what a discipled nation's government should look like? How our social services and welfare system should operate? How we should educate our children, run our banks, or make our laws?

Too many of us have fallen into the trap of accepting the separation of church and state as if it were a biblical concept. It seems like such a good idea after the corruption of the Dark Ages that brought on Luther's Reformation and the problems we face because of nations based on religious law today in the Middle East. Yet instead of tossing the Bible out of the public arena, we need to look to the Scriptures again and let the Holy Spirit teach us how to do these things as God would do them in heaven. After all, His wisdom is still relevant.

Once we start to take a fresh look at Scripture, God is going to show us how, as a Holy Nation, to begin to affect our world on a reformational level that will produce lasting transformation. Because I am not a specialist on every aspect of society, rather than try to propose solutions that I am not equipped to give, I want to prime the pump on reformational thinking in a variety of important areas. To put it in a nutshell, "We need our minds renewed (reformed) so we can be transformed." The process of becoming a Holy Nation first requires some major restructuring of our thinking.

This leads to a major point that I want to make:

Our minds need to be discipled before we can disciple a nation.

Or, to put it biblically:

If you abide in My word, you are My disciples indeed. And you shall know the truth, and the truth shall make you free (John 8:31-32).

And:

Do not be conformed to this world, but be transformed by the renewing of your mind, that you may prove what is that good and acceptable and perfect will of God (Romans 12:2).

How we see truth depends on our starting point. The war for our minds and the way we think has largely been won by the way we have all been taught to see the world. This is why I want to bring up the subject of worldview. Most of us, even strong believers, see the world through a lens polluted by humanistic thinking, and on a deeper level than we could ever imagine. Even those of us who truly believe God's Word is the final authority have had our margins moved outside of scriptural bounds by the society in which we were educated. This education has not only been in the classroom but through media and supposedly neutral programs termed as "scientific." The more I've delved into the subject of the biblical discipleship of nations, the more I've realized that my own worldview has been affected by secularistic thinking.

Let me give you an example: Once while on a trip to the state of Hawaii, we had stopped to visit with a local leader. At a meeting sometime before this, I had prophesied that Hawaii would be the first Christian state in America, and I was excited to see the level of engagement that various leaders were making with that prophecy. After our meeting, Mike and I were passing the state courthouse when I had one of those "stop here right now, there is a missing piece on your adventure to disciple nations" moments. Because we were on vacation, God had to give Mike a large measure of patience for those recurring moments.

We parked and went into the museum dedicated to the first territorial court system of Hawaii. As we read the signs, we were amazed! Hawaii's legal system had been built upon the Ten Commandments. Literally, what was legal in heaven was legal on earth.

This meant that, among other things, adultery was just as illegal as killing and stealing were. I am ashamed to admit that this gave me pause to think. I said to Mike, "Can we legislate morality in that way today?" Mike replied in his usual logical manner, "Of course, honey, we do it all the time! Why do you think it's illegal to steal?"

I stood on the spot, simply stunned. Somehow in my list of the Ten Commandments, I had allowed them to become merely moral directives, but not social laws. I was thinking of them just as secularists do, but not as God does. I had forgotten that at one time in Israel's history adultery was not only immoral but illegal. I had also subliminally accepted the notion that "whatever two people do in private is no one else's business." It hadn't occurred to me that for the sake of preserving the sanctity of marriage it wasn't God's will for a society to allow adultery. I had fallen into the thinking of sociological justice—accepting what the society as a whole believes should be illegal—rather than adhering to biblical justice. Embarrassing, isn't it? Essentially I had come to believe that certain laws of God could not be valid in our society today just because the society I lived in had decided against them.

Before you read any further, it would be good to engage both your heart and mind to become willing to make a radical shift in your thinking. To do that, ask the Holy Spirit to expose to you any way that you have been affected by secularism or any other "ism" that is ungodly. Pray with me:

O Lord,

I need Your help! I submit my whole self to You. Please, by the power of the Holy Spirit, come as a divine surgeon into my thinking. Father, anywhere that I have been taught or come to believe what is false thinking—not thinking according to Your Word and will for my life—change me. Change the way I think. Renew my mind. I do not want to be conformed to the world but desire to see Your kingdom come and Your will be done on earth as it is in heaven.

In Jesus' name,

Amen.

CAN WE FOLLOW GOD'S LAW WITHOUT FALLING INTO LEGALISM?

I am aware that this section might raise questions like: "Are you advocating putting us all back under the 613 Mosaic laws?" or "Are you proposing that we return to stoning women caught in adultery?" Of course not.

However, as I have grappled with how we deal with the Ten Commandments in our society today, let me say to you: This is a serious issue to pray and think about. Are the Ten Commandments mere suggestions to us in our societies today? If not, then how do we, in a democratic way, shift our nations' laws to reflect God's intent for our nations in this day and age? You might ask, "Why do we even need to deal with this question of adultery in society at all? Isn't that a private matter?"

As always, we need to look at this issue through a biblical lens. Westerners see very little connection between what a person does in the privacy of a home or hotel and problems in the society. However, this is not true according to the Creator's design of the earth and its inhabitants.

In order to see this according to a biblical worldview, let's examine a few passages to see what happens to the physical land of a nation when people commit sexual sin.

Leviticus 18 gives us a list of prohibited sexual acts. Among them are incest, adultery, bestiality, and homosexuality. One of the final verses of this chapter tells us:

> *Do not defile yourselves with any of these things; for by all these the nations are defiled, which I am casting out before you* (Leviticus 18:24).

In other words, the other nations were cast out of Canaan and the land given to the Israelites because they allowed those sins in their society. The passage goes on to state:

> *For the land is defiled; therefore I visit the punishment of its iniquity upon it, and the land vomits out its inhabitants* (Leviticus 18:25).

What does that mean? Just what it says: No one will be able to live in a land defiled by sin. Nothing or no one who tries to live there will prosper. The land will "vomit" them out.

There are numbers of other passages that relate to this issue of land being defiled through sin. Another powerful one is Hosea 4:1-3:

> *Hear the word of the Lord, you children of Israel, for the Lord brings a charge* [literally a legal case] *against the inhabitants of the land:* [Then the Lord states the legal case and its basis.] *"There is no truth or mercy or knowledge of God in the land. By swearing and lying, killing and stealing and committing adultery, they break all restraint, with bloodshed upon bloodshed. Therefore the land will mourn; and everyone who dwells there will waste away*

with the beasts of the field and the birds of the air; even the fish of the sea will be taken away."

Powerful! The Bible is telling us that when there is an accumulation of sin in a nation, it removes God's blessing not only from the government and the inhabitants, but creation itself!

A friend of mind, Rick Ridings, shared with me that he and other prayer warriors went to pray in the Ben Hinnom Valley in Israel. This is the site where the worshipers of Molech sacrificed babies by burning them alive. They repented for the sin done years ago by having a Jewish believer pray and ask forgiveness for the horrible atrocities committed there.

You might ask, "Why do I have to repent of the sin of my nation, past or present, that I did not commit?" Second Samuel 21:1-14 tells us that God required David to repent for the sin that the former king, Saul, committed against a tribe of people called the Gibeonites. After King David repented, the Lord heeded the prayer for the land. Also, in Deuteronomy 21:1-8 God told the Israelites to atone for the sins of His people if a person is found murdered and no one knows who did it.

I realize some of you may also be thinking, "But aren't we New Testament believers? Are we under the curse of the law?" Of course not; however, the Old Testament was the Bible for the New Testament church, and it doesn't negate how God set up creation. The good news is that God gave us, the church, the power through prayer to "redeem the land" from the effects of sin.

Several months after Rick and his team prayed in Ben Hinnom, they took a bus tour of the area. As they passed the Hinnom Valley, the Jewish tour guide said, "Since this place has been cursed because of the sin done here by the Molech worshipers, there have been no birds here for some time; however, for some unknown reason, they have returned in the past few months."

Coincidence? I don't think so. This is the biblical model for "healing the land." Second Chronicles 7:13-14 tells us:

> *When I shut up heaven and there is no rain, or command the locusts to devour the land, or send pestilence among My people, if My people who are called by My name will humble themselves, and pray and seek My face, and turn from their wicked ways, then I will hear from heaven, and will forgive their sin and heal their land.*

What is the result of our praying prayers of repentance? God will heal the land. Literally, the Hebrew says, "He will *rapha* their land." This is the same word we find in Scripture describing the physical healing of a person's body. The word *land* here is often spiritualized to mean "nation" or "region," but if you look it up, it literally means "the dirt, the earth, that stuff that we grow plants on" (my paraphrase). Idolatry also releases God's curses on the earth. Just look at Islam to see what happens when nations come under that type of religion. The land itself begins to turn to desert. I have been in nations in Africa that have become increasingly Islamic, and they tell me their rainfall has diminished dramatically since they have been overtaken by Islam.

One of the most important Scriptures on intercession also deals with the healing of land:

> *"So I sought for a man among them who would make a wall, and stand in the gap before Me on behalf of the land, that I should not destroy it; but I found no one. Therefore I have poured out My indignation on them; I have consumed them with the fire of My wrath; and I have recompensed their deeds on their own heads," says the Lord God* (Ezekiel 22:30-31).

Understanding the correlation between what happens not only to our society but all of creation is critical to how we implement God's restrictions within our legal structures.

What will this look like? The best-case scenario, of course, is that the heart of the nation is so changed through revival that the majority of the people want righteous laws. Am I suggesting that we put people in stocks and publicly ridicule them if they commit adultery? No. However, I do believe that God will give us a way to put legal sanctions upon those who commit this sin just as we already do for many other offenses.

In the United States, for example, we have laws that do not permit an adult to have sexual relations with someone under the age of eighteen, even with the child's consent. It is considered statutory rape. The military has strict limits on sexual conduct as well. Perhaps this is hard to consider because our minds have been so defiled through a secular worldview that we no longer think God's laws will work.

Neither am I advocating forcing people to convert to Christianity or taking away the democratic rights of non-Christians. The beauty of a nation based upon God's Word is that we do not persecute those who believe differently than we do, nor do we force conversions. God wants us to come to Him on our own as an act of free will, and this is why democracy, based upon the principles of God's Word, is so powerful. We are not like those who would put Sharia law (Islamic law) into place.

This is part of the reformational shift that needs to take place in our nations. We need young people who will study to become righteous judges, lawyers, and politicians who love God's Word and will seek His face on how to please Him in every area of our legal systems.

DEVELOPING A HEAVENLY PERSPECTIVE

Our individual worldviews affect the way we think, raise our children, create laws, judge morality, and administer justice. Our worldviews determine the responsibility we take for the poor and our attitudes about other nation-shaping ideologies. In order to renew our minds toward a godly worldview, we need to find out where we have been affected by thinking that is other than biblical in nature. Alvin Toffler in his book *Future Shock* says, "Every person carries within his head a mental model of the world—a subjective representation of external reality."[2] In order to understand this, you need to find out what is in your "worldview box." Your worldview box is basically your mind. In it are stored your thoughts. Those thoughts define how you see the world. (Sometimes we talk about thinking "outside of the box," which means thinking outside our current worldview. However, there is a correct "box" we should think within— one defined by a biblical worldview.)

Before about three hundred years ago, most people in the Western world had a theistic—God-centered, biblical—worldview. In this worldview, there is a direct connection between the spiritual and physical realm—with God being over all. Therefore, the society and government were in a large measure based upon a belief that whatever God said in the Bible was right. Church laws and legal precedents in common and civil law flowed from biblical and church sources. Whenever laws were written, God's Word was considered first. We will call this worldview theism.

People knew God as Creator, and His law was unquestionably obeyed, even if some did not fully understand why. If one did not obey God's law, there were consequences. People knew that hell was real and separation from God was the penalty for rejecting Him. This thinking molded actions and morality as well as the character and nature of society. God's existence was a given and served as the center that held everything together.

Another worldview came into being during the Age of Enlightenment called deism. Intellectuals accepted God in their worldview, but believed that although God created the universe, He left us free to run it. Human beings began to shift away from seeing God as the all in all in society toward the acceptance of reality as based on natural not divine law. Rationalism became the predominant philosophy of the day and the sole test for truth. In other words, if they didn't understand the "whys" of the Bible, they tossed it aside. As a result of this shift, humanity began to rationalize sin away— we were no longer guilty before God but merely victims of circumstance. This came from the teaching of Sigmund Freud.

From Freudism, we cannot argue what is right or wrong. For example, one cannot reason that it is okay to run a stop sign because we had a bad day. Why? It is the law. It is the same with God's laws. Breaking them brings consequences in our societies. Thank God though for the healing and redemptive power of prayer!

A broader worldview has come into play in the last two hundred years, however, that has done the most damage. You could call it secularism, naturalism, or atheistic materialism. It took deism one step further from God, not only saying that He isn't involved in our world but that He doesn't even exist. Reality was no longer concrete but subject to the beholder, and morality became relative. Concepts such as situation ethics and values clarification were introduced, which ultimately severed our final mooring to Bible-based morality and values. Suddenly there were no more absolutes.

To explain situation ethics in its simplest terms, we merely need to look at how it has been used in American public schools during the previous few decades. This is likely being done in a similar way around the world. (I hope readers from other nations will forgive my using more illustrations drawn from my own nation than from others. I am obviously more familiar with our story. It is my prayer that you will be able to draw from these principles to establish just societies in your own nations. The Word of God will work no matter where you live!)

In its simplest form, a teacher would tell the class that they are going to play a game—children like games. Then the teacher would tell a story something like this:

Five people were in a boat on the ocean: a pregnant woman, a priest, an old man, a child, and a sailor. The boat starts to sink because it is overloaded, and someone is going to have to be thrown out. Which one should they throw overboard? If they throw the pregnant woman off, the baby will die along with her. If the sailor goes, they won't know how to navigate the boat. The child would surely die. Perhaps the priest should offer himself. The old man has lived his life.

Discussion ensues. The teacher tells the pupils there are no right or wrong answers. The answers they give will be right for them, based on their values. This is called values clarification—all absolutes are taken away. There is no higher authority in the picture to pray to and ask for guidance. Such an option is not even proposed. Where are the boundaries? Other scenarios are given as the days go by, such as who should starve if there isn't enough food.

Where did I first hear this taught? Strangely enough, in my Christian university's teachers' education classes.

The frightening danger in this is that there are no absolutes. If we obey the laws of morality only when it seems good for us, lawlessness will ensue. Everything is fluid in this kind of society except for one thing—whatever you think is best for you. Thus the ultimate decisive value becomes selfishness—"watching out for number one" becomes the basis for all ethics and morality.

Shockingly enough, the founder of the theory of situation ethics was Joseph Fletcher, a former Episcopal priest. Later in life he became an atheist and denied God altogether. His book *Situation Ethics: The New Morality* was written in 1966. He was also the president of the Euthanasia Society of America (later called the Society for the Right to Die). In addition, he was a member of the American Eugenics Society and the Association for Voluntary Sterilization.[3]

Imagine this man's philosophies being interjected into our school systems. This was just one part of an insidious plan to erode the population's belief in God and eliminate absolutes from our society.

Ironically, a Beatles song during this time period summed it up: "All You Need Is Love." Fletcher taught that apart from love there are no unbreakable rules. There are no absolutes or maxims. This might have worked, but then he went on to use human love as his basis for this and threw God's love out the window. Love became subjective, and the Bible was no longer seen as God's law but an ancient text that could be disregarded when modern reasoning showed a better way.

It is chilling to think that God's commandments are thought of as general "suggestions" put into the context of selfish human love. Being higher than God's commands leaves us without boundaries or signposts to guide our path. With this mindset, each person, based upon their feelings of love, makes up their own ethics and values.

J.I. Packer has a fascinating article on what he calls situationalism, the belief system that has come out of situation ethics. In it, he makes a powerful point:

> No situation ever faces us with a choice of evils; the traditional view to the contrary is one more product of the mistaken "intrinsic theory." "The situationalist holds

that whatever is the most loving thing in the situation is the right and good thing. It is not excusably evil; it is positively good."[4]

Therefore, we could say that from the situationalist's viewpoint, moral compasses have no true north. It is a fluctuating north called "love." The only trouble with this is that we also have a sin nature that distorts that love in the same way that setting a magnet next to a compass will change its readings. God's love, being the good father-love that it is, knows that we His children must have boundaries called "law" to mitigate against our sin natures. We must know there are absolutes so that the distortions created by our sin nature and selfish desires are counteracted; otherwise, we lose our way because our compass readings—based on feelings and justifications—are off.

Taking Fletcher's thoughts to their logical progression, we would eventually have to accept that there is nothing that is absolutely sinful. This is where society stands today. If we do not understand how far we have fallen in our ethics, we will never be able to disciple our nations.

My earthly father, Albert S. Johnson, wrote a Scripture passage in the flyleaf of my Bible. It deals with the subject of situation ethics well:

For the Word that God speaks is alive and full of power [making it active, operative, energizing, and effective]; it is sharper than any two-edged sword, penetrating to the dividing line of the breath of life (soul) and [the immortal] spirit, and of joints and marrow [of the deepest parts of our nature], exposing and sifting and analyzing and judging the very thoughts and purposes of the heart (Hebrews 4:12 AMPC).

Only the Word of God gives us the answers to questions such as whether or not a mother should abort her baby even though it seems that she cannot raise another child. The loving choices, obeying God and choosing to preserve life, are one and the same. The world would tell us that we need to consider the mother solely and not the unborn child. However, according to God's Word, aborting a baby is not a loving thing to do; it is being disobedient to God and is in fact an evil choice to take an innocent life. God is the Creator and the Giver of life; therefore, we do not have the right to take that life away.

Love needs God's laws to keep it true, for love—God's love—is the fulfillment of the law (see Rom. 13:10).

The Importance of Absolutes

I recently had an insightful discussion with a young Korean woman who had only been a Christian for a short time. She said to me, "Cindy, what is wrong with two men or two women loving each other when they are not hurting anyone else?" In other words, she wanted to know if love is the rule that makes everything right.

After praying a moment, I replied to her, "I don't have a personal opinion. Let's see what the Creator says in the Bible—the manufacturer's handbook." Then I read Romans 1:24-27 to her:

> *Therefore God also gave them up to uncleanness, in the lusts of their hearts, to dishonor their bodies among themselves, who exchanged the truth of God for the lie, and worshiped and served the creature rather than the Creator, who is blessed forever. Amen.*
>
> *For this reason God gave them up to vile passions. For even their women exchanged the natural use for what is against nature. Likewise also the men, leaving the natural use of the woman, burned in their lust for one another, men with*

> *men committing what is shameful, and receiving in them-selves the penalty of their error which was due.*

She immediately understood the intent of God for His creation and could see the answer to her question without my saying another word.

Hold this clear word found in the above Scripture passage up against the teaching of Fletcher in his book *Moral Responsibility*, in which he writes, "Sex is not always wrong outside marriage, even for Christians."⁵ God's Word says that sexual sin—adultery, fornication, and homosexuality—is sin, period. It isn't relative whether or not it is "true love" as the world thinks. Any expression of love that conflicts with God's Word is not true love. Putting our own ideas of love over God's warps His truth and changes it into a lie. Following such lies will eventually lead to death, not the joy and freedom Fletcher promises.

Perhaps this would be a good time to stop and ponder your own personal belief systems. Have you fallen into this kind of situational thinking? Ask the Holy Spirit to reveal to you whether your margins of morality are more defined by the society in which you live or by God's Word.

The philosophies of Fletcher and those like him thus became the bridge between deism (God made the world and spun it off into space, having nothing more to do with it) and secularism (God has nothing to do with us because He never existed in the first place). Fletcher was, at the time, a "Christian liberal theologian," though ultimately he was a secularist in sheep's clothing. This is where much of the church is today, even though we might protest it vehemently. Most pastors no longer preach about sin at all. Rather, it is assumed that we all know right from wrong—but do we?

One important piece that must be put into place in order to radically shift the worldview of nations is for the church to teach sound doctrine again. We need to lay the foundations of truth for our people. We need to be Bible-centered rather than "seeker sensitive," or we will soon trade seeing people saved for being politically correct.

We need to teach the Word. We need to make it clear from our pulpits what God considers sinful in His world. The teaching gift was highlighted in the 1970s in the church but has fallen from popularity in recent decades. We must come full circle—not only giving inspirational talks but line-upon-line teaching. If we do not, there will come a wave of deception greater than anything we have previously seen, and our churches will get swept up in it without even a whisper of protest.

Not only do we need to teach the Word in churches, but we need to release godly values into society by becoming influencers in the marketplaces of our nations, allowing God's wisdom to reign. We need to disciple our children to become leaders, godly leaders, who can clearly teach that the Bible has more wisdom for creating a just society than any other source of knowledge or system of morality.

As believers, we have been greatly lacking in training future generations to lead our nations. Other ideologies have not been remiss in this. The Communist Party has spread their doctrine around the world. If communists could influence whole continents in their belief system, why can't we? Communism is the counterfeit of Christianity. God has a plan for the nations; we need to care enough to find out what it is.

After the fall of communism in Eastern Europe, some Christians were put into power, but they didn't know how to run a government. Eventually the people reelected the communist hardliners because at least they could put some kind of governmental structure into place.

This is because as part of their indoctrination they studied how to overthrow and form governments. They had a presubscribed system to follow; the Christians did not.

There are some at this point who are still saying, "But won't things change if we simply have national revivals?" Yes, that is a major starting point, but it is not enough. While evangelism is one of the keys to discipling nations, we must also be prepared to disciple them into "Holy Nation thinking" after people are saved. This discipleship must include the renewing of their minds with the Word of God in areas our churches and few Christian colleges have not gone, addressing the seven mountains of society. There are some exceptions to this as some schools, such as Arizona Christian University in the Phoenix area, teach on how to be a reformer on all these sectors of society. They are surely a prototype for colleges.

My husband and I have talked about how we went to Sunday school every week as children and were taught the basics of Scripture, yet many churches today do not have graded discipleship training at all. It is often a hit-or-miss proposition and does little to teach a biblical worldview. Churches do not generally know how to disciple with a kingdom mindset. We have been great at teaching people to be servants, but lousy at teaching those servants to reign as Joseph did in Egypt. How is it we have the keys to the kingdom, but still have yet to open the windows of heaven for our nations today?

In the following chapters we will look at these areas of society and start to explore what they might look like if they were rebuilt in the image God has for each of them. The underpinnings of Scripture were kicked out from under our societies many years ago, but God will help us reposition them. We need to learn to fight the just fight for the minds and souls of our children, schools, institutions, and nations.

Chapter Five

TEACHING NATIONS

MANY OF US know the verses known as the Great Commission by heart while we continue to miss what it really says. We hear: "Go out and make converts." But it actually says: *"Go...and make disciples of all the nations...teaching them to observe all things that I have commanded you"* (Matt. 28:19-20). Let's put that into today's language: "Go out and teach students God's ways and wisdom." Or you might para-phrase it: "Teach them the true biblical worldview."

Is this talking about starting Sunday school classes wherever we go? I don't think so. While we need Sunday schools for disciple-ship, we also need to be where the students are—in our schools, col-leges, and universities—as well as teaching our children at home. Yet instead we have given the job of teaching our nations to our govern-ments and accepted the teaching of humanistic naturalism as science. Now this godless philosophy has invaded every subject.

It didn't used to be that way. Only a century ago it was the Christians who built the schools, wrote the curriculum, and taught our children how to live. Less than half a century ago, our American schoolchildren still started the day with prayer in the classroom. How did things change so much?

As we look around the world today, can we say that there is any nation that is being taught to observe all that Jesus commanded us? Why not? I admit that the thought of teaching a nation is a daunting one. However, understand that every single believer has a calling to do just that, and each of us is critical to seeing it fulfilled. You have a place in changing nations whether you are a mother at home with your children, a corporation executive, or a plumber!

If this is shocking to you, I can relate. Before God showed me this, I was in the same boat. I read my Bible for years, actively witnessed to people on a one-to-one basis, but never realized that I had a responsibility not only to disciple but to teach nations. Why didn't I see that as my role?

For one thing, it didn't occur to me even to think on that scale. Evidently, it hasn't occurred to a large part of the body of Christ. How could this be? We have for the most part accepted a cultural worldview without a second thought.

Part of this is due to something called dualism, which stems from Greek thinking. Most of us who have been educated through Western educational models see everything through the filter of Greek thinking. Dualism categorizes the world into that which is spiritual—pure and good—and that which is material—corrupted and bad. According to one form of dualism, a person's physical body is a "prison house," an impediment to the person's pure spirit. Another form of dualism can be found in Plato's thought; he talks about spiritual "forms," which are purer and more real than their material "copies" on earth. Dualism is also very individualistic rather than communal. So those of us affected by this philosophy first take Jesus' command to make disciples as a spiritual command but not a material one, thinking we only need to teach about being converted and living spiritually, and then only relating it to individuals, not communities or nations. We have so painted ourselves into a corner that we have little relevance to the rest of society anymore.

As a result, we read Matthew 28:19-20 as "Go into all the world and evangelize individuals and teach them to obey the spiritual lessons of the Bible." While, of course, we must do this, as God wants all to be saved (see 1 Tim. 2:4) and live fulfilled lives, we miss the actual biblical mandate to go into the world and teach nations how to observe the morals, ethics, character, principles, and doctrines of the Bible. While we may allow the world we know on Sunday to affect the way we function as an individual Monday through Saturday, we realize none of our responsibilities to teach society as a whole. In fact, we are so far from this understanding about educating, or discipling and teaching nations, that very few believers see the relevance of bringing the teachings of Jesus into every part of their societal world—i.e., business, government, science, law, education, and the like.

In his book *The Church in the Workplace*, Peter Wagner quotes Dennis Peacock to illustrate how this affects us in the area of business and finance:

> Dualism has polluted evangelical Christianity in grievous ways. The marketplace was "carnal" because it dealt with "earthly things" like business and money. Adultery was properly viewed as sinful, but the worldly realm of economics was viewed, like politics, as some kind of "neutral zone" where Christianity had no real place trying to affect the system of economics, production, management, or distribution. Hence, no Christian ministry was possible in that realm.[1]

Darrow Miller calls this thinking "evangelical Gnosticism." Simply put, there is a hard line between the spiritual and natural worlds—they have little or nothing to do with each other. Certain aspects of life are seen as sacred or spiritual—such as faith, theology, and missions—and are put in the "Sunday box."

Physical aspects of life—such as feeding the poor, science, government, the laws of society—are considered of less importance and are therefore put in the "secular box." Thus pulpit ministers get put into the "spiritual box" while everyone else who doesn't preach from a pulpit gets put in a "secular box."

RENEWING OUR WORLDVIEW

In biblical thinking, however, this is not so. The Old Testament roundly rejects dualism. Hebraic thought starts with the premise that God is the One who created the physical world (see Gen. 1:1); therefore, the physical world is a gift from God and is good. Since our physical bodies are also gifts from God, they are also good because God created and pronounced them so. Even the distinction between the spirit and body—or spirit, soul, and body—is indistinct. Just as God is One—though Father, Son, and Spirit—so are we.

God addresses nations as well as individuals, and what was intended for the synagogue was also meant for the marketplace, schoolhouse, laboratory, hospital, museum, theater, political discussion at the corner cafe, or anywhere else people are gathered. According to a biblical worldview, it is spiritual to be a scientist or a science teacher, because God created the world. The Creator gave us the love of beauty and art, so we should also express that through painting, music, and drama. We His children, of all people, should bring order out of chaos into every aspect of life.

Even though we should be conforming the world to God's biblical pattern through teaching them to observe all things He has commanded us, we not only do not know how to do this but we don't even see it as our role. Look again at John 3:16: God loves the world, and He wants us to love the world as well. We need to return to our Genesis mandate to be stewards of all creation. We must participate with the Holy Spirit not only in bringing individuals to salvation in Christ (something of critical eternal importance) but also in fulfilling our role as caretakers and administrators of everything in it. When we do that, we begin to understand how to teach the nations as God intended us to.

Is this an overly optimistic goal? No. In my travels I have seen nations take very positive strides toward adopting God's intentions for them. Argentina, as I mentioned earlier, is just one of them. I can truthfully say, however, that I do not know of one nation where believers have fulfilled their biblical mandate. The United States saw this to a degree at its foundation, but that heritage has been left in the dust by many in society today.

It is disheartening to think of the fact that while we have not succeeded in teaching whole nations, there is a group who has—the humanists. This has at least happened in the Western world. Other nations have been influenced as well because most of the intellectuals of these nations have received their education at universities that have bought into the humanist worldview.

How did this happen? It can be better understood if we follow a diabolical strategy that began a long time ago in England with a man named Erasmus Darwin, the grandfather of Charles Darwin. He was a medical doctor who came from a very wealthy family line that was related by marriage to the Wedgwood family (of fine-china fame). It is interesting to note how many of the original propagators of evolutionary thought were influential people of wealth.

Erasmus was a member of the Lunar Society, a group of fourteen prominent industrialists, natural philosophers, and intellectuals who met regularly in Birmingham, England from 1765 to 1813. The Lunar Society recognized the Bible as the greatest single obstacle to the achievement of its socialistic aims. Their primary intention was to remove the church from a position of power in Great Britain.[2]

They knew that they would never be successful in a direct attack on the church and so evolved a plan to discredit the story of creation and thus the Bible as well. To obtain their goal, they would also purport that God was not the Creator of the world. They reasoned that people would come to the conclusion that if God wasn't the Creator, then none of His laws were in effect either. The church in Great Britain was the keeper of His laws, and so by discrediting the Creator, they would discredit the church.

Looking back, it was a deviously brilliant plan. Erasmus, one of the founders of the Lunar Society, wrote a book entitled *Zoonomia*, which laid the groundwork for what his grandson Charles would claim in his later work *On the Origin of Species* (1859), subtitled *by Means of Natural Selection or the Preservation of Favored Races in the Struggle for Life*. Karl Marx and Adolf Hitler totally bought into his thinking, and the result was the murder of more than six million Jews during the Holocaust and tens of millions more under communism.

Other contributors from the Lunar Society fed into this evolutionary sabotage. A key player was a man named James Hutton (1726-1797). He rejected the idea of a literal worldwide flood, calling it a fabrication by what he considered uneducated Jewish writers. A geologist, he believed the earth evolved over a longer period of time than the six thousand years biblical scholars traditionally calculated as the maximum age of the earth from biblical accounts.[3]

The thinking of Hutton and Darwin is called naturalism. Naturalists believe that any "phenomena or hypotheses commonly labeled as supernatural, are either false or not inherently different from natural phenomena or hypotheses."[4] According to this interpretation we cannot know anything from a supernatural source, i.e., from God.

In the Beginning

One of the key shifts in our thinking away from theism (God is the Creator and ruler of the universe) to humanistic naturalism occurred as a result of the teaching of evolution. This is the doctrine that our children are subjected to every day in their schools. If they answer on a test that God created the world, they fail the test. In addition, The Discovery Channel, Animal Planet, cartoons, movies, and other forms of media and entertainment feed this kind of thinking to our children with few of us even noticing.

Dennis Lindsay, the president of Christ for the Nations Bible Institute in Dallas, Texas, has spent a good portion of his life researching creation science. In fact, he has written a series of twelve books on the subject. He cites the Scopes Trial in 1925—an event fictionalized in the play *Inherit the Wind* and which legalized the teaching of evolution in public schools—as a major turning point in American education. Prior to this time, the biblical foundations built into the United States by the framers of the Constitution were taught in schools. Evolution was still being debated.

Yet even in that day it would have been unimaginable to think that prayer would be taken out of schools less than thirty years later, in 1962, and Bible reading would be forbidden in the classroom by 1963. In 1925, most people still scoffed at the idea that human beings had apes as close cousins, let alone one-celled animals that "just happened" in primordial sludge. It was still generally believed that God created us as human beings and we are not the same as animals.

Why then has evolution become so fashionable, even though it makes no more sense now than it did a century ago? There is really no more fossil evidence for evolution today than there was in 1925. Dennis Lindsay says in his book *The ABCs of Evolutionism*:

> All fossils which have been found are either 100 percent ape, 100 percent men, or 100 percent fraud. Absolutely no in-between creations have been found. This has become so painfully obvious that even the evolutionists are reporting more and more about the lack of evidence that surrounds the issue of the transitional form—the missing link.[5]

For example, an article in *The Dallas Morning News* in 1994 entitled "On Ancestral Trails: Conflicting Evidence Muddies Path for Scientists Tracking Human Origins," said:

> Because of the lack of evidence, controversy surrounds just about every step of human evolution, from Lucy's [a fossil the article was discussing] first footfalls to the Neanderthals' last gasp about 35,000 years ago.
>
> "It's not at all like high-energy physics, for instance, where one has a body of highly developed theory to work with," said Philip Rightmire of the State University of New York at Binghamton.
>
> Instead of well-defined theory, human evolution has a handful of fossils and a pile of contradictory genetic and archaeological evidence about the human past.[6]

(Christ for the Nations Institute has the Creation Science Museum on their campus that is open to the public for those who wish to study this further.)

WHEN PHILOSOPHY IS PASSED OFF AS SCIENCE

So what has happened to our societies? How is it that science—the supposed study of the natural universe based on factual observation—suddenly feels it has the right to speak spiritually about whether or not creation had a Designer? Make no mistake—the claims of naturalists about the origins of the universe based on evolution require far more "blind faith" to accept than the book of Genesis. Yet since the indoctrination of naturalism has been so complete, we can no longer simply begin evangelizing with John 3:16. Scriptures such as this presuppose that God exists and that He created the world. Today, in order to evangelize, we must begin with Genesis 1:1: *"In the beginning God created the heavens and the earth."*

I was once witnessing to a homosexual on a plane. He was a really pleasant young man, and we had a wonderful conversation. We were talking about the laws of society. While we did not speak of homosexuality directly, it was understood that our topic was whether or not the lifestyle was right or wrong.

I posed a question to him in the midst of our sharing: "Do you have a father?" "Yes," he replied. I went on, "When you were growing up, did your father have rules that you needed to obey as his son?" "Yes," he replied. (He was on the way home to visit his family.) "Why did he do that?" I queried. "Well," he answered, "I suppose because he was the authority and had that right."

The next thing I said was, "Why do you think we have laws in our society?" He replied, "Because we need them to keep things from deteriorating into anarchy." I countered, "Are those laws meant to be obeyed?" I gave examples such as running red lights, and then went on to stealing and murder. "Of course," he answered with a grin.

"Well then," I proceeded, "let's say there is a God and He is the Creator of you and me and everything, as the Bible says. If that is true, then He made the universe, and the Bible says He makes the rules." "Okay," he said. I went on, "He is the authority and the lawgiver as the Creator, and He wrote His rules down in the rulebook, the Bible. What do you think happens when we don't obey His rules?"

From that point I could see understanding in his eyes. "Have you ever seen the movie *The Passion of the Christ*?" I asked. "My friend wants me to watch it with him," he replied. "Well," I said, "here is what that movie is about, and this is what you do to respond." I then proceeded to give him the plan of salvation.

The next thing that happened was so sweet. He smiled and pulled a book out of his backpack, "Cindy," he said, "have you ever read this book? My partner is reading it and gave it to me." It was *The Purpose-Driven Life* by Rick Warren. My point is that he didn't have any frame of reference for John 3:16, so I had to go back to Genesis to witness to him.

JUST ANOTHER ANIMAL

Because of Darwinism, we are now at a place in many nations where Christianity is resented and opposed—even in America. Social Darwinism declares that man is only a higher form of animal—an evolved ape—rather than God's crowning creation with a soul. Yet they also believe in progressivism, that man will get better and better through time until we enter a utopian state of world peace. We have *"changed the glory of the incorruptible God into an image made like corruptible man—and birds and four-footed animals and creeping things"* (Rom. 1:23). Because of this, God has given us up to "uncleanness," "vile passions," and a "debased mind" (see Rom. 1:24-28).

Some animal activists believe that people who cause the death of an animal should have the same treatment in court as those who murder humans, because they believe we are all only animals at differing stages of evolution (please don't misunderstand; I am an animal lover and object to the mistreatment of animals by anyone). Desmond Morris' *The Naked Ape* (1967) popularized this thinking. This is startling, because there is no evolutionary connection that gives us evidence that this is so.[7]

One of the reasons that slave owners could say that they were born-again Christians and still own humans was that they believed that the Africans they captured were subhuman and did not have a soul. This deep sin goes beyond racism and is akin to Darwinism. In their minds, they could do what they wanted with their slaves because they believed themselves to be a higher form of animal. The Ku Klux Klan believed in white supremacy and reasoned they could murder black people because they believed African Americans were little better than animals. The teaching of evolution today can easily reinforce the root of such racial hatred.

This thinking could also be backed up by Darwin's natural selection. Only certain races and people were the fittest and more evolved. Not many people are familiar with the subtitle of Darwin's *On the Origin of Species*, mentioned earlier in the chapter: *Preservation of the Favoured Races*. Unfortunately, the idea of eugenics was not only popular among the Nazis at the beginning of the twentieth century. Many notable Americans, including presidents, supported it.

While this chapter is not meant to present a complete teaching on evolution versus creation science, this discussion is a key building block to understanding how we arrived at where we are today—societies taught by humanists with an agenda to completely eradicate God. Humanism is the belief that we can make things right in the world through human goodness that is universal in all humankind. Humanists do not believe in the God of the Bible and believe that people are basically good and will choose the right way through our own innate goodness. What is right is rationalistic and based upon societies' needs as a whole rather than our Creator's absolutes.

Social Darwinism has now evolved into humanism and has become like a sociological computer virus that has destroyed the fabric of societies across the face of the earth. As we go further into areas of biblical justice, you will see how it has affected us. While some of the references will be to the United States, those reading from other nations will be able to apply the biblical understanding to their countries and judicial systems.

HUMANISMS GROWING INFLUENCE

How have humanists been able to propagate their ideology? The answer is simple: through the public educational systems. Humanists know how to teach nations. By teaching the children, they are discipling our countries into their belief system. This is what has happened in the United States and throughout Europe.

Changing the U.S. into a nation based on humanism rather than Christianity was well planned. It began with a document called the Humanist Manifesto in 1933. The preamble to the manifesto is startling to the Christian reader. Even more startling is the fact that one of the signers is known as the "Father of Modern American Education," John Dewey. Here are a few quotes:

> The time has come for widespread recognition of the radical changes in religious beliefs throughout the modern world. The time is past for mere revision of traditional attitudes. Science and economic change have disrupted the old beliefs. In order that religious humanism may be better understood we, the undersigned, desire to make certain affirmations which we believe the facts of our contemporary life demonstrate.

After these beginning remarks, they state fifteen points not only of their beliefs but their plan. Here are some of the points:

> First: Religious humanists regard the universe as self-existing and not created.
>
> ...Fifth: Humanism asserts that the nature of the universe depicted by modern science makes unacceptable any supernatural or cosmic guarantees of human values.
>
> ...Ninth: In the place of the old attitudes involved in worship and prayer, the humanist finds his religious emotions expressed in a heightened sense of personal life and in a cooperative effort to promote social well-being.
>
> Tenth: It follows that there will be no uniquely religious emotions and attitudes of the kind hitherto associated with belief in the supernatural.[8]

Forty years later, in 1973, Paul Kurtz and Edwin H. Wilson wrote the *Humanist Manifesto II*. Edwin H. Wilson was also a writer of the original Humanist Manifesto. He graduated from Meadville Theological School in 1926 and was an ordained Unitarian minister. Paul Kurtz, who has published over eight hundred articles and edited more than forty-five books, is Professor Emeritus of Philosophy at the University at Buffalo in New York as of this writing.

With the second manifesto, there was a shift from religious humanism to secular humanism. Here is one of its preface statements:

> As in 1933, humanists still believe that traditional theism, especially faith in the prayer-hearing God, assumed to live and care for persons, to hear and understand their prayers, and to be able to do something about them, is an unproved and outmoded faith. Salvationism, based on mere affirmation, still appears as harmful,

diverting people with false hopes of heaven hereafter. Reasonable minds look to other means for survival.[9]

The points of the manifesto are shocking. While they believe that we should not allow exploitive forms of sexual expression, they also express that they do not wish to prohibit, by law or social sanction, sexual behavior between consenting adults. They also express the right to abortion. In the area of sexuality, they state this:

> We believe that intolerant attitudes, often cultivated by orthodox religions and puritanical cultures, unduly repress sexual conduct.[10]

EDUCATION LOSES ITS VALUES

You may be surprised, as was I, to learn that John Dewey—who, for all I knew, had only invented the Dewey decimal system (a system of filing hard-copy books in libraries)—was a subscriber to the tenets written in the Humanist Manifesto I. Because of his influence as an educational innovator, a dark and evil force entered the school systems—not only of America, but throughout the world. Dewey was a lecturer who spoke to educators across the face of the earth.

One of the major changes Dewey made in education was to catch it up with the industrial revolution—education was no longer to teach people how to live but how to function in order to get a job. People's worth was no longer determined by integrity and what they contributed to their community but how employable they were and what kind of job they could get. This fundamental change knocked the pillars of moral education out of the classrooms, and it only made sense that the expulsion of prayer and Bible reading would eventually follow. Religion became an obstacle rather than a help and foundation for true knowledge. Science and democracy would become the new religion.

Here is one example of the kinds of lectures Dewey gave:

> But of one thing I am quite sure: our ordinary opin-
> ions about the rise and falling off of religion are highly
> conventional, based mostly upon the acceptance of a
> standard of religion which is the product of just those
> things in historic religions which are ceasing to be cred-
> ible. So far as education is concerned, those who believe
> in religion as a natural expression of human experience
> must devote themselves to the development of the ideas
> of life which lie implicit and are still new science and
> are still newer democracy. They must interest themselves
> in the transformation of those institutions which still
> bear the dogmatic and the feudal stamp (and which do
> not?) till they are in accord with these ideas. In perform-
> ing this service, it is their business to do what they can
> to prevent all public educational agencies from being
> employed in ways which inevitably impede the recog-
> nition of the spiritual import of science and democracy,
> and hence of the type of religion which will be the fine
> flower of the modern spirit's achievement.[11]

This philosophy is at the root of every public school district in
America, as well as the systems of other nations. The accepted religion of our education system has become humanism, and its pulpit
is the public school classroom.

Dewey's School and Society laid the foundation for the transformation of the schools into hotbeds of humanism. Another of his
statements shows this agenda:

> I believe the true center of correlation on the school
> subjects is not science, nor literature, nor history, nor

geography, but the child's social activities. I believe that the school is primarily a social institution. All the questions of the grading of the child and his promotion should be determined by reference to the same standard. Examinations are of use only so far as they test the child's fitness for social life.[12]

Some nations already give a "social grade" in order to be given the right to move into certain influential buildings and to get jobs. The United States seems to be moving that way and we pray that this doesn't happen.

Humanism has become mainstreamed through progressivism and naturalistic theory, which omit any reference to God or religion. By the 1960s, these ideologies controlled the power bases of education at all levels. In other words, they transformed society through education.

Catherine Barrett, 1972-73 president of the National Education Association (the nation's largest teachers' union), addressed the membership in 1975, saying this:

We will need to recognize that so-called basic skills, which currently represent nearly the total effort in elementary schools, will be taught in one quarter of the present school day. The remaining time will be devoted to what is truly fundamental and basic—time for academic inquiry, time for students to develop their own interests, time for a dialogue between students and teachers; more than a dispenser of information, the teacher will be a conveyer of values, a philosopher.[13]

In a 1972 keynote address to members of the Association for Childhood Education, Harvard psychiatrist Chester M. Pierce challenged public schoolteachers to lead the way in transforming the next generation:

> Every child in America entering school at the age of five is mentally ill…because he comes to school with certain allegiances to our Founding Fathers, towards our elected officials, towards his parents, toward a belief in a supernatural being, and toward the sovereignty of this nation as a separate entity. It's up to you as teachers to make all these sick children well—by creating the international child of the future.[14]

Contrast this with what we know about early education in America from the textbooks they used in the 1700s, such as *The New England Primer* with a reported two million copies sold. Among their other lessons, the children would be taught the prayer:

> *Now I lay me down to sleep,*
> *I pray thee, Lord, my soul to keep;*
> *If I should die before I wake,*
> *I pray thee, Lord, my soul to take.*[15]

Another well-loved textbook was *The McGuffey Reader*. It is estimated that one hundred twenty million McGuffey Readers were sold between 1836 and 1960. They still sell at a rate of thirty thousand a year.[16]

William Holmes McGuffey (1800-1873) was teaching at Miami University in Oxford, Ohio, when his friend Harriet Beecher Stowe (author of *Uncle Tom's Cabin*, one of the death knells for slavery in the U.S.) recommended him to a publisher to write four graded readers for primary school students. These readers helped form the morals of the nation. They taught character issues—that lying, cheating, stealing, and using foul language were bad. This strengthened the moral fiber of the nation. McGuffey Readers played an important part in American history.

Let's put these books and values up against those being taught in the major universities of America today. The University of Michigan offers a course for English 317: "How to Be Gay: Male Homosexuality and Initiation." University of Maryland students can choose "Selected Topics in Lesbian, Gay, and Bisexual Literature." UCLA has offered classes such as "Lesbian and Gay Literature Before Stonewall." Other universities offer courses in sexual politics and gay and lesbian musicology.[17] The plan? The "gaying" of America. This is part of the agenda of those who framed the Homosexual Manifesto. While it is prefaced as satire, it has been followed as doctrine by those with an agenda for the "gaying" of the nations.

This plan extends all of the way down to grammar schools and the kindergarten level. Five-year-olds are being encouraged to read books in the North Carolina school districts with a homosexual agenda. One that has been approved is *King and King* by Linda de Han and Stern Nijland. It is the story of how a king marries a king. There are more than forty children's books circulating with a homosexual theme like this.

As I am writing, it has been fifty-four years since what was called in America "the summer of love" (1967) in San Francisco. It was really the summer of promiscuity and sin that released a wave of rebellion against God into society. After college, many of those who participated in this movement became teachers in the universities of the nations and taught their ideologies to their students. We are seeing the fruit of this in society today.

ATTACKING THE STRONGHOLDS

Satan is a strategist. Only a few years before that "summer of love," Bible reading and prayer were officially removed from public schools. From then on millions of children stopped hearing God's truths in school every day, acknowledging God as the Creator and Ruler of the universe. It is not hard to see a connection between these events.

As we look at the educational system here in America—where the influencers of the nations send their children to be prepared for life—we should consider this warning from Romans:

> *For the wrath of God is revealed from heaven against all ungodliness and unrighteousness of men, who suppress the truth in unrighteousness, because what may be known of God is manifest in them, for God has shown it to them.*
>
> *...Men, leaving the natural use of the woman, burned in their lust for one another, men with men committing what is shameful, and receiving in themselves the penalty of their error which was due.*
>
> *And even as they did not like to retain God in their knowledge, God gave them over to a debased mind, to do those things which are not fitting; being filled with all unrighteousness, sexual immorality,* [and] *wickedness* (Romans 1:18-19,27-29).

So what are we to do? Many in America have taken the avenue of homeschooling their children or sending them to private Christian schools. Those are good and viable choices that are even now being threatened in the United States. However, what about all the other children in our nations? What is our moral responsibility toward them? How do we, indeed, teach nations and reverse what has happened in our schools? There are parents in other nations who have been arrested for homeschooling their children. Why? Because they believe the government only can adequately teach values to their children—among other things.

And what about nations that don't have private Christian education? What about the poor who cannot afford to send their children to private schools or buy curriculum for homeschooling? Do we simply abandon these kids to social Darwinism and humanism? First of all, we need a prayer strategy. Chapter Nine, "Legislating in the Heavens," details how to begin to break the strongholds that have developed through false teaching.

Second, we need to be informed. What are your children being taught? Look at their textbooks and listen in on their classes as an observer. Take a tour of the school's library.

Third, find out what the universities in your area are teaching. If you find something that is shocking in the courses, let others know and make a formal complaint to the university. Find out who funds the schools and write them. Protest to your government leaders if you find something that is offensive.

Fourth, get involved in the system. By this I mean, encourage Sunday school students to become public schoolteachers. Children should be raised with the idea of becoming missionaries to the school systems. Teachers, God will anoint you to be change agents in children's lives around the world. You are called as holy revolutionaries to your school.

Fifth, churches need to get involved with the public schools. Find out when school board elections are taking place and unite with the pastors and other leaders in your area to elect godly people to have control of what goes on in the school district.

I want to encourage pastors to understand that you have a critical role to play in the worldview of your people. The pastors of churches in every nation have always, historically, been a voice for righteousness. Appoint a liaison from your church to keep you informed about the schools in your area. Make an appointment with the mayor or other top government official in your city and talk with your congregation about what you have learned.

There is a great underground movement taking place of Christian parents who are informed about the conditions of the public schools. Private Christian schools and the homeschooling movement around the world are keys to changing the nations, but we must also infuse the public schools with righteousness to transform nations.

If you are currently a schoolteacher, find other teachers who would be willing to pray together. God wants to reverse the Humanist Manifesto and its tentacles over the face of the earth. Accept the call of God as a reformer in the school system. Form prayer groups in your schools.

Pastors, adopt the teachers of your area in intercession. At the same time, all of us must pray for revival to break out across the nations of the earth. We must teach our children both in church and in the home that they are called of God to reform their nations according to God's societal rule book—the Bible. After that we will begin to see righteousness rise up in our lands, and we will fulfill the biblical mandate to "teach nations to observe all things that He has commanded us."

Chapter Six

WHO'S THE JUDGE?

SEVERAL YEARS AGO I was preparing to preach at a Christian conference in Mar del Plata, Argentina. I could not seem to discern what God wanted me to preach that night. I was "suffering for the message," as I put it—walking the floor and praying for direction.

As I paced back and forth in my hotel room, a strange thought came to me. Let me put it in the context of reforming a nation. I had been going to Argentina since 1990. Each year God would give me some kind of word for the nation. Many of them had been quite radical. For instance, one year I gathered a group of major leaders and gave them the prophetic word that the economy of the nation was going to collapse. I had previously had a vision of people rioting in the streets of Buenos Aires, trying to get their money out of the banks. This was hard for the leaders to believe, but yet it happened in 2001.

Since that time, the Lord had given me prophecies that would help to reconstruct the nation. The thought that came to me in the beautiful seaside city of Mar del Plata was that I should tell the people that they needed to start paying taxes to the government.

This may not sound all that radical to those of you in the United States. Most people here know that we all must pay our taxes or be thrown in jail. The Internal Revenue Service moves quickly to prosecute those who do not. While there are still people in the United States who try to avoid or fail to pay their taxes, the vast majority faithfully pay their taxes as they are due. But that is not the norm in many developing countries, including Argentina.

That night I stood to speak in the large former opera house. As I peered up at the balconies, I spoke about God being the great judge of the universe and that in order to please God, we need to be upright not only in our dealings with the Creator but also with earthly governments. I said, "You might not pay taxes because you believe the government is corrupt and doesn't deserve your money. However, the Bible is clear on the subject in Romans 13:1-2,7."

> *Let every soul be subject to the governing authorities. For there is no authority except from God, and the authorities that exist are appointed by God. Therefore whoever resists the authority resists the ordinance of God, and those who resist will bring judgment on themselves. ...Render therefore to all their due: taxes to whom taxes are due, customs to whom customs, fear to whom fear, honor to whom honor.*

At the end of the service I asked all of those who did not pay taxes to stand. I was stunned at the response. The conference was mainly for church leaders and dedicated Christians, yet the majority of those in the audience stood up. These beloved people were very honest. Many came forward and made a vow to the Lord to begin paying the government what was due. They repented with deep sincerity before the Lord concerning this issue. We then prayed for them that God would give them the faith to continue doing what was right in this regard.

A couple of years later, I was talking to one of the men who work with the poor in that country. He gave me this testimony:

> When I heard you share how God had spoken to you that one of the problems we have in Argentina is that the church members do not pay taxes to the government, I was smitten with conviction. I was one of those who paid our people "off the books." This way I didn't have to pay taxes to the government on their wages.
>
> The night that you gave us the prophecy to pay taxes, I decided to change. I went home and gathered my leaders and told them from that day I was going to pay taxes plus keep their wages the same. This required a lot of faith on my part; however, from that day God has supplied.

My friend went on to say that not only did he pay the staff and his taxes, but God had given a great increase to his work among the poor as well.

Other pastors went back to their churches and preached to their people that they needed to pay their taxes. Is there any correlation between the action the church took and that there was an economic turnaround? I believe strongly that the blessing of the Lord came upon that nation because the church started acting in a righteous manner. In fact, God gave me a prophecy after that time that the nation would supernaturally recover from their economic collapse, and it happened! One of the nation's top economists is a Christian and says that the nation's remarkable financial recovery has none of the usual economic indicators that occur with such a dramatic recovery from an economic disaster. There is a "supernatural" factor that they did not figure into the index! Sadly, a new government has come into power in Argentina, and the economy has now taken a dramatic downturn. We are believing for this to change!

IS THERE ANY RIGHTEOUS?

What is the correlation between paying taxes and a nation changing? It is called biblical justice—when we act biblically, the righteous judge of the universe fights on our behalf. Much like when Abraham interceded for Sodom and Gomorrah, God was willing to spare these cities' destruction for the sake of a few righteous people. The same is true for nations today because "righteousness exalts a nation" (Prov. 14:34). This marriage of righteousness and justice are vital to the reformation of a nation.

While ministering in the African nation of Nigeria, I was perplexed by the apparent disconnect between the sheer numbers of Christians and the nation's lack of righteousness. I had heard of the famous prayer meetings there where millions of Christians would pray together, but the nation did not seem to be changing in any positive way. Finally, I queried a few of their top business leaders: "How does Nigeria have so many believers, but yet have a reputation as one of the most corrupt nations on earth?"

Systemic corruption (meaning bribery and nepotism infecting every area of daily business and governmental interaction) was ruining the nation. They all knew about it, but no one had any solutions because it is a huge, tangled problem. So I proposed to them, "Why don't we begin today by writing an ethics covenant between church leaders? Let's make a list of certain practices that you will and will not participate in." They each agreed. Time will tell the results. Thank God for the many believers in Nigeria and other parts of Africa who are praying and working to break this spirit of corruption.

Where there is corruption it is not possible to receive true justice. I have heard numbers of stories where the lawyers for a case would place a large sum of money between the pages of the files they presented to the judge trying their case, and the judge would then decide in favor of the person who offered the largest bribe in various nations. How can this be?

Justice will only be served where there is the mooring of biblical righteousness. There can be no just ruling without absolutes and ethics. Otherwise, the results will either be according to how much money it takes to "buy off" the judge or determined by "sociological justice"—in other words, whatever is consistent with the current subjective morals of the society.

If we are to disciple and teach nations, we must set ethical standards for how we will conduct ourselves and what we will allow, not by what the world thinks is acceptable or by what makes our lives easier but by what is truly righteous. We cannot expect our nations to act any better than we do ourselves. We cannot be reformers when we have no higher standards than those around us, no matter how small we think the issues before us may be. Our worldview will be reflected in our actions, and if we don't act according to a biblical worldview then, quite frankly, it is not what we truly believe.

SETTING A NEW STANDARD FOR JUSTICE

One day as I was teaching in Nigeria, I felt led to have each person write down the ways that they have not obeyed the law. I gave examples, such as driving on the sidewalk, paying bribes, accepting bribes, etc. Right in the midst of the sermon, I started to feel the conviction of God! "Cindy," the Holy Spirit admonished, "you can't tell the people they need to repent before you repent of your sin of breaking the law!"

Frankly, this puzzled me. I hadn't killed anyone or broken into a store and robbed it. Yet the Holy Spirit went on with this rebuke, and I felt the fear of the Lord grip me as I was confronted with my own sin: "What about your sin of speeding?" (Now about this point, some of you are going to wish you had never read this chapter!)

He continued, "What do you think those signs with numbers on them posted by the U.S. Department of Transportation mean?" Oh, this was starting to hurt! Those signs are the law, not suggestions—and they are meant to be obeyed. Then He said, "I want you to repent to all the church here in Nigeria and tell them that you are a sinner!"

I hate to confess that my feeble excuse was, "But Lord, everyone does that! We make jokes about it in the U.S.!" Even as I spoke, it sounded pretty weak. What could I do? I had no choice but to obey the voice of God. So I publicly repented.

I have to confess that I still struggle with this at times and have a very rebellious foot that I have to keep a close watch on! I grumble and think things like, *Well, I am late. I have to go faster. After all, it's not my fault that I'm late!* When I was growing up, my mother often repeated the adage "Two wrongs don't make a right." (My friend, if you are guilty as charged, just repent of your sin so we can move on. Please don't stop reading! But also don't think that you can be a world-changer without acting righteously! Besides, why should I be alone in my snail-paced driving? My husband has always driven the speed limit, and it has always irked me—I had to repent of that too!)

NO RIGHTEOUSNESS, NO JUSTICE

Many of us might not feel bad about breaking the law, yet we still want to receive justice when we are wronged. In order to disciple and teach nations, we need to maintain higher standards than those around us. This is because we serve the Judge and Lawgiver of the universe, and He maintains absolutes. Something is either right or it is wrong.

Scripture is very straightforward in this regard. It gives us the understanding of who God is in Isaiah 33:22:

> *For the Lord is our Judge, the Lord is our Lawgiver, the Lord is our King; He will save us.*

In order to really understand what this verse is about, it is important to contrast the modern-day idea of justice to a biblical understanding of justice. Biblically, we need to marry the concept of justice with God's righteousness if we are to truly understand it.

According to *Nelson's Bible Dictionary*, the Bible speaks of "doing justice" (see Ps. 82:3 and Prov. 21:3) whereas we speak of "getting justice." Doing justice is "to maintain what is right" or "to set things right." Justice is done when honorable relations are maintained between husbands and wives, parents and children, employers and employees, government and citizens, and humanity and God. *The New Unger's Bible Dictionary* amplifies this by saying that "man in his relation to man is to reflect the justice or righteousness of God." Justice is not only respect for the rights of one's fellow man regarding life, property, and reputation, but in its broadest sense also includes the proper recognition of each individual's duty toward God.

Law and situation ethics are complete opposites. There can be no law based on situation ethics. Law without an ultimate judge and lawgiver can only deteriorate into anarchy or tyranny. Law without the fear of the Lord turns our cities into police states.

At one time, European nations were governed solely by the arbitrary laws of kings. The kings were the law. Then in 1644, Samuel Rutherford wrote his *Lex, Rex, or The Law and the Prince*. What is the concept in *Lex, Rex*? Very simply, *the law is king*. Rutherford also argued that the king and civil government must be based on God's law—the Bible—and that all power and right to govern is from God. If the king and the government disobey the law, they should be disobeyed.[1] He had this to say about tyrannical government: "a power [whether] ethical, politic, or moral, to oppress, is not from God, and is not a power but a licentious deviation of a power; and is no more from God, but from sinful nature and the old serpent, than a license to sin."[2]

In other words, any government not from God will fall prey to man's sinful nature. Tyrants sometimes make unusual laws. A pastor in Iraq once told me that Saddam Hussein made a law that it was illegal for anyone but him to eat a banana.

Ultimately, God is the Lawgiver, the King, and the Judge. The major shift that has taken place through the influence of humanism, among other things, is that God's laws are no longer ultimate. For humanists, humanity—including our debased thinking and desires—has become king of the universe. Right and wrong has thus been subjected to rationalizations of our fleshly passions and weaknesses. Liberty no longer stands for the freedom to do what is right but the freedom to do whatever one wants.

Samuel Rutherford's *Lex, Rex* was outlawed in both England and Scotland. In fact, at the time of Rutherford's death, the parliament of Scotland had decided to execute him. However, he died before the sentence could be carried out.

THE ONLY POSSIBLE FOUNDATION FOR A JUST SOCIETY

A society cannot be just unless it is centered on God's absolute laws. This is a crucial point we must grasp as believers today. There are certain things that our society may say are legal on earth, but they are not legal in heaven. They are "legal" according to the laws of the nation, but the great Judge of the universe says they are not. A law cannot be just if it is not righteous. Unbiblical laws need to be abolished, or our societies will suffer for the sin they allow.

Without the marriage of righteousness and justice, humans make their own arbitrary laws. We take away the foundation of God's laws and the foundation of allowing the kingdom of God to be established on the earth. Psalm 89:14 and Psalm 97:2 say that righteousness and justice are the foundation of His throne— He has built His authority upon them and His rule is established by them. If we don't understand God's perspective, then we will not have a clear definition of what is just. God Himself trusted Abraham with the knowledge that He was going to destroy Sodom and Gomorrah because Abraham understood this marriage of principles:

> *For I have known him, in order that he may command his children and his household after him, that they keep the way of the Lord, to do righteousness and justice, that the Lord may bring to Abraham what He has spoken to him* (Genesis 18:19).

Scripture tells us that David was a good ruler because he administered justice (*mishpat*) and righteousness (*tsadaqah*) to all his people (see 2 Sam. 8:15). The New King James Version renders these two words *judgment* and *justice*. According to the *Enhanced Strong's Lexicon*, *mishpat* means a "sentence, decision (of judgment)," "justice, right, rectitude (attributes of God or man)," as well as someone getting what is "due (legal)."[3] *Tsadaqah* means "righteousness" in "government," "of God's attribute," "in a case or cause," "as ethically right," and "as vindicated," and also figuratively "prosperity (of people)."[4]

Another powerful passage that speaks to us strongly on the theme of reformation, discipling, and teaching nations is Isaiah 9:7:

> *Of the increase of His government and peace there will be no end, upon the throne of David and over His kingdom, to order it and establish it with judgment* [mishpat] *and justice* [tsadaqah].

An interesting thought on this passage is if His government and peace will increase, who makes that happen on the earth? Think of this in light of Matthew 6:10. We, as stewards of the earth called to disciple nations and teach them to observe all He has commanded us, are mandated to see that righteousness and justice increase on the earth. It is up to us who believe and will answer that call.

JUSTICE FOR ALL

There are at least sixty-four verses concerning the marriage of righteousness and justice in Scripture. A number of them pertain to justice for the poor and oppressed. We will examine some of those in the chapter dealing with biblical economics.

Godly laws release justice into the earth. Governments that are based upon biblical law are blessed and prosperous. In fact, as we just saw, one of the definitions of righteousness is "prosperity (of people)," meaning when a society is just, it prospers.

When God's laws are in place, justice will be colorblind. Justice is not the "survival of the fittest race" as Darwinism would tell us. There is no place for racism in God's kingdom. In God's eyes all human beings are created equal and are His crowning creation. Therefore, every person regardless of economic status or skin color deserves justice—simply because it is right. God, the great Judge, is surely deeply grieved when there are inquities among people simply because of the color of their skin! I personally believe that racism is a sin. God loves color! He made His children different colors and shades of color because he thrives on the different peoples of the earth. In God's justice, I am praying for a day that racism will end.

In fact, God's justice extends beyond the verdicts of courts; it also includes restitution to the wronged person. Zacchaeus understood this and after his encounter with Jesus said, *"Look, Lord, I give half of my goods to the poor; and if I have taken anything from anyone by false accusation, I restore fourfold"* (Luke 19:8).

Biblically, the law of restitution only required an extra 20 percent to be given in restitution for extortion (see Lev. 5:16; Num. 5:7). Yet because Zacchaeus had an experience with the living God, he did more than justice demanded and acted righteously.

A nation's worldview concerning justice is extremely critical to its economy. In examining the subject of law and government, I saw a common thread between the prosperity that both the United States and England have experienced and the bedrock of English Common Law written by William Blackstone. I love the story of Blackstone. It gives me great hope and faith for those who might otherwise be written off as having little potential to change a nation.

Blackstone, at thirty-five years old, seemed a failure in life. He was overweight and chronically ill. Filled with self-doubt, he took the podium in an Oxford lecture hall on October 25, 1758 to address the students. He apologized for the plan he was going to present as "crude and injudicious." However, the series of lectures he began that day was later published as *Commentaries of the Laws of England* and dominated legal discourse in England as well as other nations for more than a century.

The commentaries were printed in four volumes. Book IV covered "Public Wrongs." It discussed crimes and punishments, including wrongdoings against God and religion. Blackstone believed that man-made laws were like scientific laws—they had to be discovered. God had set them both into existence in His creation in a similar way. It was the place of governments to discern them just as it was the place of scientists such as Isaac Newton to document them.[5]

In his 1941 book *The Mysterious Science of the Law*, Daniel Boorstin wrote of Blackstone's *Commentaries* that no other book except the Bible played a greater role in the history of America's legal framework. The blueprint of the nation's judicial system was found in Blackstone, and Blackstone's blueprint was the Bible.

Abraham Lincoln was greatly affected by Blackstone's *Commentaries* while on his own path to becoming a lawyer. Lincoln at first thought that he would become a blacksmith because of his lack of formal education. He saw himself as a poor candidate for law and thought that he had "slim prospects" for success. The two books that most influenced his life, however, were the Bible and Blackstone's *Commentaries*. It was Blackstone's writings that laid the foundation in his mind that all just laws must originate from biblical precepts.

The wording of the Declaration of Independence is based almost directly on Blackstone's phrases, such as "the self-evident," "unalienable Rights of people" granted by the "Laws of Nature and of Nature's God." Compare this wording with the first precept of the Humanist Manifesto that John Dewey, the so-called "Father of American Education," signed: "Religious humanists regard the universe as self-existing and not created."

As an American, I have to say with great embarrassment before God, *O Father, how far we have fallen away from Your law and precepts embedded in our foundations.* I don't use the words embedded in our foundations lightly. They are critical. America's success as a nation is dependent on the fact that we based our government, society, and early education on the laws and precepts of the Bible.

In order to see how far we have eroded the Christian roots of our society, we need to take a look at historic precedents. For instance, in 1824 the Supreme Court of Pennsylvania, in the case of Updegraph v. The Commonwealth, indicted Updegraph for blasphemy against God, using Blackstone's legal definition:

> Blasphemy against the Almighty is denying His being or Providence or uttering contumelious [insulting] reproaches on our Savior Christ. It is punished at common law by fine and imprisonment, for Christianity is part of the laws of the land.[6]

Contrast this with the rulings in more recent court cases (Stone v. Graham, 1980; Ring v. Grand Forks Public School District, 1980; and Lanner v. Wimmer, 1981): "It is unconstitutional for students to see the Ten Commandments since they might read, meditate upon, respect, or obey them."[7]

WE MUST RETURN TO FIRST PRINCIPLES

The United States needs not only a nationwide revival but a nation-changing reformation. We need to go back to the foundations of English Common Law and to the principles upon which our forefathers founded our nation. In the past it was not uncommon for a Christian judge to lead a condemned man to the Lord from the bench!

You may have read of John Quincy Adams as well as President Thomas Jefferson attending church services when they were held in the Capitol building. Note this entry from Adams' diary: "Religious service is usually performed on Sundays at the Treasury office and at the Capitol. I went both forenoon and afternoon to the Treasury."[8] The entry was dated October 23, 1803.

How have we fallen so far from our founding principles as a nation? Many Christian lawyers and judges have not studied the subject of biblical justice and so do not have this bedrock as a paradigm for their thinking. Rather they have studied case law and constitutional law. I know these are required to pass the bar exam, but there is a higher court than any earthly one—it is the court of heaven.

Scripture tells us about the law of the kings. This is what was required for each king:

> *It shall be, when he* [the king] *sits on the throne of his kingdom, that he shall write for himself a copy of this law in a book, from the one before the priests, the Levites. And it shall be with him, and he shall read it all the days of his life, that he may learn to fear the Lord his God and be careful to observe all the words of this law and these statutes, that his heart may not be lifted above his brethren, that he may not turn aside from the commandment to the right hand or to the left, and that he may prolong his days in his kingdom, he and his children in the midst of Israel* (Deuteronomy 17:18-20).

How can one fulfill their calling as a lawyer or judge without being versed in God's laws? God is the ultimate Lawgiver. The king makes the laws of the kingdom, Congress makes the laws of our democracy, but it is still God who makes the laws of the universe.[9]

IT HAS TO START IN OUR OWN HEARTS

Years ago I was teaching in Uganda, and suddenly I knew that God was giving me a key to reforming that nation. As I stood before the audience of nearly ten thousand pastors, I told them what God had given me to say to them: "There are some of you here who take up offerings supposedly for orphanages or other good causes, but instead of using the funds as you have said, you use them to build yourself a house or send your children to private schools. Others of you siphon money from the church treasury."

Before I could say more, however, I noticed that my interpreter had stopped speaking. He was choked up with tears. I whispered to him, "Are you all right?" He was a precious man of God, and I couldn't imagine what was troubling him.

He replied, obviously quite broken, weeping, "Mama Cindy, I am so sorry. I think that most, if not all of us, do those things! All our fathers in the Lord did those things, and we did not know they were wrong!"

Shocked and heartbroken, I continued, speaking to the whole assembly now, "Please understand, this behavior is lying and stealing, and it breaks two of the Ten Commandments." At the end of my sermon there was a wave of deep repentance, and we wept together as they declared that there was a new generation of leaders in the nation that would not participate in such corruption. I believe Uganda is seeing the fruit of this repentance today. Great leaders have risen out of that group who are now releasing righteousness across the land.

I believe with all of my heart that God is anointing a new breed of leaders across the face of the earth who will both reform and, if need be, oppose laws that break the law of God. One of the greatest issues that must be dealt with is abortion. In 1973, the Supreme Court of America ruled abortion legal in the United States by a five to four vote. Since that time more than sixty-four million babies have been aborted in the U.S. That is roughly more than eight times the population of the Dallas/Fort Worth area where I live. So many innocent children murdered because they were inconvenient shows the magnitude of this silent holocaust. It is blood we will have to answer for in heaven. Liberals and feminists say that a woman has the right to do what she wants with her own body, but does she? If that were so, why do we stop a woman who tries to commit suicide?

This is where understanding the marriage of righteousness and justice is critical. A woman might say, "I shouldn't have to take care of a baby I didn't plan to have. I shouldn't have to deal with a pregnancy when I can have an abortion." In their minds, their action is just and right. Their situation seems to justify their actions. But is it ever right to murder an innocent child?

Justice cannot be done through situation ethics; we must do what is righteous.

Abortion is only right if we do not believe that God is the author of life and that it begins at conception. In the minds of many who abort their children, they are only disposing of tissue, but most of us know better than that now.

One of the main reasons we are even dealing with the problem of abortion is because we have judges who believe justice is sociological, not godly. They believe righteousness is based upon the will of the people and society's current accepted ethics rather than the law of God. In fact, we are naïve if we think there is a neutral judge. They all rule to a degree according to their own belief systems, even though they may say they do not. Only a godly judge can step out of his or her own selfish perspective enough to judge fairly every time.

One radical youth movement sprang up to fight this evil in the United States before the 2004 presidential election. A young man had a dream that he and his friends put wide red tape across their mouths with the word *Life* written across it and stood in silent vigil in front of the Supreme Court building until Roe V. Wade was overthrown. The resulting group is called the Justice House of Prayer, or JHOP. This 24/7 youth prayer movement has its prayer room right around the corner from the Supreme Court. They intercede every day and will do so until abortion is again illegal in the United States. Not only do they intercede in the prayer room, but every day they also stand and pray in front of the Supreme Court building. They are there whether it rains or snows, in the cold of winter and heat of summer. They have a cause and a mission—to see the end of legalized abortion in this country. As they pray, they petition the highest court in the universe, the court of heaven. Their prayers will avail.

It is my dream that many of you reading this book will live to see the day when abortion is again illegal. There may be another just cause you can fight for, using the JHOP as your godly example.

ANSWERING THE CALL

As I travel around the world, I often hear lawyer jokes. Most of them are about corruption and greed in the profession. We desperately need godly young men and women to follow the call of God to be legal reformers, redeeming the areas of law and justice. Thank God, many around the world are redeeming their judicial systems and overthrowing corruption. They understand the marriage of righteousness and justice.

God is calling all of us to see justice done for the poor, needy, widows, orphans, and unborn children. One day we will look into the faces of our children and grandchildren and tell them the stories of the battle for the courts. I can hear the sweet voices of future generations ask with unbelief, "Grandfather, did mothers and daddies really kill innocent babies when you were a child?"

On January 17, 2005, I stood on the steps of the Lincoln Memorial with a group of teenagers, hearing the call to reform our nation across America. It was Martin Luther King Jr. Day, and I thought of the famous speech by Dr. King from this very location to tens of thousands of listeners, his voice resounding with the words "I have a dream."

As I looked out across the grassy mall that stretched all the way to the Capitol building, I began to declare:

> There will be a day when little schoolchildren from all across America will give their nickels and quarters to build a memorial on this mall to the unborn. The memorial will be built by a righteous nation to show their grief for the holocaust of children lost because of abortion, thereby saying, "Never again will this nation kill its babies in the womb."

Chapter Seven

PUTTING THE GOVERNMENT UPON HIS SHOULDERS

GOD HAS A plan for each of His children. Deposited within every man, woman, and child there is a destiny, a purpose, and a reason each was born. However, many live and die without ever realizing the "why" of their existence.

It is my prayer that as you read this book, you will feel the drumbeat of God's call to be a change agent to your generation. God is looking for people willing to answer the call to disciple the nations. We need passionate leaders willing to be influencers for God. True freedom and development depends on Christians taking their places as change-makers in positions of authority as well as service.

Nations will not change without Christians in those nations becoming major influencers in their governments. The will of God cannot be done on earth as it is in heaven without His people being righteous voices calling for laws that release His justice. As we turn back the pages of history, it is easy to see the immense struggle that has taken place since the fall in the garden for the control of our nations. God the Creator makes the rules, but He has given into our hands the release of His righteousness on behalf of all creation. When we step back from that role and become the church shut off in isolation, there is no one to speak for righteousness in the public arenas.

Sin brings corruption, discrimination, and injustice on the earth. God's ambassadors, however, release righteousness, equity, and justice. Governments need elected officials who will legislate on behalf of God's goodness or they will eventually crumble. In each generation, one can see the anointing of God upon leaders who have the courage to stand up as voices of righteousness to fight inequity, racism, poverty, corruption, abortion, and other social ills. One such warrior of righteousness was a young man named William Wilberforce. God is looking for men and women just like him to be His voice in their generation.

WILLIAM WILBERFORCE AND FRIENDS

I doubt anyone would have seen a lion of governmental reformation in the future of young William Wilberforce. His father died when he was nine. He suffered poor health and poor eyesight all his life, and from a very young age had to wear a steel frame to support his back. One would more likely have seen him as a candidate to remain in a home for invalids than as a statesman in Parliament, but God doesn't see people as we do.

Through his hardships, William learned the one quality I have found to be a hallmark of reformers—perseverance. Sometimes we think we need a massive amount of faith to function as change agents; however, I am convinced that faith comes to the faithful. While "the just shall live by faith" was the cornerstone verse of Luther's Reformation, to me, that means "the just shall live by faithfulness." Great faith is best exemplified by the simple act of getting out of bed every morning and obeying God no matter how our bodies feel, what emotions we are battling, or what people are saying about us. The great reformers—Wilberforce among them—kept going even though they were terribly tempted to quit at times. One thing Wilberforce had in his favor was his voice and education. He was both eloquent and charismatic.

Imagine yourself as a twenty-one-year-old, walking into Congress or Parliament as an elected member. That is exactly what Wilberforce did. He was the youngest member of Parliament ever elected. Both his grandfather and his uncle included him generously in their wills. God had His hand in the timing of the transfer of that wealth, because young William used it to help finance his campaign to run for public office.

While studying at Cambridge, he became friends with another young man destined for greatness whose name was William Pitt. Pitt was only twenty-four when he became prime minister of the United Kingdom. God would use the friendship of these young men to help abolish the slave trade in the British Isles, although at times they parted company on other issues. One could say they were a bit like David and Jonathan in the Bible.

Wilberforce had a profound conversion experience and believed that Christianity was the only basis upon which civilized society could be built. After Pitt became prime minister, he approached Wilberforce in a legendary conversation beneath an old tree on Pitt's Holwood estate about his willingness to become involved in the parliamentary campaign to abolish slavery. Pitt had urged Wilberforce to read an exposé on the slave trade, and when he did, Wilberforce was cut to the depths of his heart by the inhumanity of the business. Wilberforce was only twenty-eight years old at the time, and although he agreed to propose an anti-slavery bill immediately, due to illness he would not be able to introduce it for another year. However, the conversation had changed Wilberforce forever. Afterward, as his life's purpose, he believed God had called him to "two great objects: the abolition of the slave trade and the reformation of manners."

Allow me to interject a personal note here: Never underestimate the power of friends and mentors to inspire their disciples toward a particular call. Peter Wagner did this for me on a number of occasions. At times a conversation with a friend has inspired me personally to take on a role in a project that I otherwise would never have tackled.

There are occasions when God requires that we take on a task of great magnitude without our having any idea how long it will take or at what cost. In great endeavors of this kind where the soul of a nation is at stake, it can take much longer than we think to be accomplished. Wilberforce's struggle for the abolition of slavery would take more than four decades, with many setbacks and a few false victories along the way. In 1789, he gave a moving address[1] that established his place as the leader of the abolitionist movement in Parliament, but when it came time to vote on the resolution, more than half the members of Parliament were absent, and the bill failed. Time and again, William felt like quitting, but each time God encouraged him to continue his righteous cause.

In fact, the last letter written by John Wesley, in 1791, was to Willberforce, supporting his anti-slavery campaign. Here is a portion of the letter the famous revivalist wrote to encourage Wilberforce:

> Unless God has raised you up for this very thing, you
> will be worn out by the opposition of men and devils;
> but if God is with you, who can be against you? Are all
> of them stronger than God? Oh, be not weary in well
> doing. Go on, in the name of God and in the power of

His might, till even American slavery, the vilest that ever saw the sun, shall vanish away before it. That he who has guided you from your youth up, may continue to strengthen you in this and in all things, is the prayer of

dear Sir, your affectionate servant
JOHN WESLEY (24 February 1791)[2]

The letter speaks to all reformers down through the ages to give them hope and strength for the fight against injustice.

COMING TOGETHER TO FULFILL GOD'S MISSION

Wilberforce had other allies in his battle concerning the abolition of slavery. A group of leaders who were warriors of the cause moved to an area of London called Clapham and formed a community that is often referred to as the Clapham Group. While not everyone involved with the movement was a member of Parliament or lived in the community, there was a core group who lived in close proximity to one another and went to church in the parish pastored by John Venn. It was to become one of the most influential parishes in England. In his book *The Wilberforce Connection* Clifford Hill quotes Michael Hennen:

Never have the members of one congregation so greatly influenced the history of the world. The effect of their prayers and actions not only profoundly altered the religious and social life of this country [meaning England], it was also felt in Africa, in the West Indies, in India and in Australasia.[3]

John Venn himself was a revolutionary as a rector. He helped start schools for the poor and insisted that his whole parish have smallpox inoculations. As a child he was quite shy. (Oftentimes we look at the little ones in our society according to a limitation, such as shyness or sickliness. However, God doesn't see children according to their health challenges or weaknesses but as great reformers in the making!)

In a fascinating social weave, the members of the Clapham Group proved to be world-changers in conviction and deed. Their decision to live in close proximity helped them work and pray together to influence the transformation of their nation and see the slave trade abolished in the British Empire (in 1807) and eventually the emancipation of all British slaves (as it happened, just three days before Wilberforce's death in 1833)—not to mention the fact that they truly enjoyed one another's company! They were in covenant not only in mission but in their love for each other and for each of their families.

Lady Knutsford's *Life and Letters of Zachary Macaulay* gives us a glimpse into the lives of the group:

> Regarding every member as forming part of a large united family, behaving toward each other as members of such a family, they treated each other's homes as their own, taking with them as a matter of course their wives and children; they kept together for their holidays and while in London arranged to meet for breakfast or dinner to discuss their many common concerns. The weight of continual business was lightened and cheered by sharing it with congenial companions.[4]

While I am writing this, I am thinking of some of my good friends and our relationships. One moment, some of my girlfriends and I are laughing and trying on shoes, and the next moment we may be planning a prayer meeting to change a nation. What fun!

This reminds me of the first question of the Westminster Shorter Catechism (1648) which begins:

What is man's chief end?

The answer:

Man's chief end is to glorify God (see Ps. 86), *and to enjoy Him forever* (see Ps. 16:5—11). (See also Psalm 73:25-28.)

I hope this doesn't offend anyone, but one of my mottos in life as I mentor young leaders is "Work hard! Play hard!" (This advice should be mixed together liberally.) We are to enjoy God and each other's company in work and in play!

All told there were 112 members of Parliament in the Clapham Group. Of course, not all of them lived in the community. There was an inner circle of around thirty who were dubbed "The Clapham Saints" and who had a greater allegiance to biblical principles than to their party affiliations. These saints met together in the home of John Thornton, where they sought the Lord for direction through worship and prayer.

In addition, the Clapham Group had members who were in professions such as banking and law, others did research, and others were church leaders. But they all worked together to reform the nation. Note the mix of ministers in the church and the marketplace! It took a team to bring the change!

A key influencer of the Clapham Group was an Anglican rector named John Newton. Newton had at one time been a slave-ship captain. After Newton returned from the sea to England, he found Christ and became involved in the anti-slavery movement, even giving evidence against it to the Privy Council (sort of like testifying before a Congressional committee in the United States). Early in Wilberforce's career, John Newton encouraged him to go on with the call to overthrow slavery. Newton is best remembered as a hymn writer, the most famous being the beloved "Amazing Grace." We all need pastors who are voices into our destinies.

We must see a mix of anointings today from all sectors of society to overthrow evil and corruption in our nations. No one sector of society can disciple and teach their nation and be reformers on their own. If Matthew 28:19-20 is ever going to be taken to a practical level, we must form new groups that meet together across the lines of pulpit ministry, government, and the marketplace (remember, whatever God calls us to do in life is our ministry) to change our nations and fight injustice in every area and on every level.

One of the Clapham Group's great successes was the use of publishing to release a moral conscience into the nation (as I am praying this book will do!). Hannah More, a leading writer and educator—and as far as I can tell, the only visible woman in leadership in the group—wrote tracts, beginning in 1795, which became famous and were known as the *Cheap Repository Tracts.* Another Clapham member, Henry Thornton, financed the publishing of them, and they sold two million copies during a time when there were only eight million people in the whole nation![5]

I believe that what these reformers did, working toward the establishment of a just government, was what the Bible is speaking about when it says that we are to be salt, light, and a city set on a hill:

> *You are the salt of the earth; but if the salt loses its flavor, how shall it be seasoned? It is then good for nothing but to be thrown out and trampled underfoot by men.*
>
> *You are the light of the world. A city that is set on a hill cannot be hidden. Nor do they light a lamp and put it under a basket, but on a lampstand, and it gives light to all who are in the house. Let your light so shine before men,*

that they may see your good works and glorify your Father in heaven (Matthew 5:13-16).

CONSTITUTIONAL GOVERNMENT

Matthew 5 could be considered part of Jesus' constitutional preamble for His followers. We are called to be a collective voice of influence. That means through voting in democratic elections, taking places of leadership in our communities, and standing up for righteousness no matter our station or occupation. Wherever we are placed as Christians, our light should dispel the darkness.

It is important to know that the Bible has patterns for the proper formation of government. This is why we must not only read Isaiah 9:6-7, which talks about the increase of God's government in the earth, but be a part of making it happen.

> *For unto us a Child is born...and the government will be upon His shoulder. And His name will be called Wonderful, Counselor, Mighty God, Everlasting Father, Prince of Peace. Of the increase of His government and peace there will be no end, upon the throne of David and over His kingdom, to order it and establish it with judgment and justice from that time forward, even forever. The zeal of the Lord of hosts will perform this* (Isaiah 9:6-7).

Here are a few of the basic tenets of government found in the Bible:

Representative Government

One of the first plans that God gave Moses after leaving Egypt was how to establish a representative government:

> *"Choose wise, understanding, and knowledgeable men from among your tribes, and I will make them heads over*

you."...So I took the heads of your tribes, wise and knowledgeable men, and made them heads over you, leaders of thousands, leaders of hundreds, leaders of fifties, leaders of tens, and officers for your tribes (Deuteronomy 1:13,15).

Since the tribes would already have chosen leaders, God gave Moses the perfect system in a tribal society for governance.

Judicial System

Moses, under God's guidance, then proceeded to establish a judicial system for the Holy Nation:

Then I commanded your judges at that time, saying, "Hear the cases between your brethren, and judge righteously between a man and his brother or the stranger who is with him. You shall not show partiality in judgment; you shall hear the small as well as the great; you shall not be afraid in any man's presence, for the judgment is God's. The case that is too hard for you, bring to me, and I will hear it" (Deuteronomy 1:16-17).

The Separation of Powers

Three branches of government function are derived from Isaiah 33:22:

For the Lord is our Judge, the Lord is our Lawgiver; the Lord is our King; He will save us.

In the United States, these are the executive, the legislative, and the judicial branches. Other nations, such as the United Kingdom, Canada, and Australia, have this separation of powers under a monarchial system, which have parliaments and prime ministers. This separation of powers is crucial because of one main element— as humans we are sinful creatures and need checks and balances.

THE BIBLE IS THE PATTERN

The Bible is the pattern for government in the earth. John Wycliffe, in 1382, said of his new translation of the Bible into English: "This Bible is for the government of the people, by the people, and for the people."[6]

The translating and printing of the Bible into the language of the people was one of the main catalysts for reformation. As people began to understand the will of God in society, they began to look at their nation through the lens of Scripture and measure it according to that standard.

We can never afford to overlook the importance of Scripture. One must not only learn to read God's Word but read God's world through the filter of His Word. Anything that doesn't line up with His will on earth is our responsibility to change by discipling and teaching nations the true importance of God's law and government.

GOD WORKS IN COMMUNITY GOVERNMENT

The only governmental systems that work on the earth are those based upon biblical principles. God is the King of the universe, yet He has given into our hands the ability to read His Word and put it into practice. We also must understand the nature of humanity from God's perspective and the deceptive power of our sin natures. Governments must have checks and balances; otherwise, the temptation of corruption and cronyism will be too much for its officials. Look at communist nations and dictatorships. Where there is no accountability, justice is soon lost as government officials look to serve themselves rather than the people.

God works in relational community rather than autocratic rule. He even exists in community within Himself as the Father, Son, and Holy Spirit! As we are salt and light, we will transform our nations into cities set on a hill, and that is only possible if we work together to establish a voice of moral clarity in our nations just as the Clapham Group did in England.

God manifests His goodness through us as His ambassadors on the earth. Godly government releases creativity, beauty, grace, and peace. Wicked governments founded on humanistic, Marxist principles only become more and more corrupt when not measured against the righteous standard of Scripture. The effects of communistic thinking washed the beautiful colors from the buildings in Russia and replaced them with drab, gray monoliths.

The effects of godless government are powerfully described in Deuteronomy 30:15-18 (NIV):

> *See, I set before you today life and prosperity, death and destruction. For I command you today to love the Lord your God, to walk in obedience to him, and to keep his commands, decrees and laws; then you will live and increase.*
>
> *...But if your heart turns away and you are not obedient, and if you are drawn away to bow down to other gods and worship them, I declare to you this day that you will certainly be destroyed.*

Without God's values and moral agendas in our governing bodies, corruption and discrimination creep in through the misuse of power. Lord John Dalberg-Acton's famous dictum still applies today: "Power tends to corrupt, and absolute power corrupts absolutely."[7]

IDEOLOGICAL PATTERNS

It is critical for us, as believers, to be students of history so we can not only see God's rule in the earth, but also the patterns of thought that need to be broken through intercession in order to heal our nations. Let's peer back together at the pages of history and examine the difference between what happened in England and France in the eighteenth century.

Throughout its history, England was affected by the teaching of reformers such as Wycliffe, Wesley, Whitefield, and Wilberforce and the Clapham Group, as well as the printing and distribution of the King James Bible, while France did not have any such influence. The power of the written Word and the Great Awakening that happened earlier in that century saved England from a bloody revolution within its own borders on the heels of the one they had just lost in America. France, however, faced one of the bloodiest revolutions Europe ever saw. The major difference between the two nations at this time was that one had a biblical worldview and the other's was based on Jean-Jacques Rousseau's nature versus society writings.

Rousseau saw a fundamental divide between society and human nature. He contended that man was instinctively good when living in a natural habitat (the state of all other animals, and the condition of humankind before the creation of civilization and society), but was corrupted by living in society with other human beings. He believed that we were originally kindly "noble savages," and it was only when we became more developed and interdependent that inequity crept into our natures. This teaching of the "noble savage"—or that we would be sinless if we lived in a completely natural environment—is prevalent in the thinking of much of society today. People believe that we are inherently good and born without a sin nature at all.

Rousseau felt that government was brought into being by the rich and powerful to "trick" the general population. Because of this, human societies were fraudulent and manipulative forms of associating from the very beginning, and societies formed by the wealthy and powerful had to be set free by the "politics of redemption"—the idea that politics can be the means not only of creating a better world but also of transforming human nature and creating "the New Man." It was not that people needed to have new hearts to exhibit goodness and justice, but to be delivered from external morals and social institutions such as family, community, and church. The state would step in and take over for these antiquated conventions and deliver their citizens into a new political utopia.

He thus called on reformers to set people free from the chains of institutions, laws, customs, and traditions. He gave no moral principles on how to accomplish this liberation or govern the state's ambitions in "freeing their populations" from the institutions of society. Thus the leaders who embraced this philosophy were some of the greatest despots of human history—Robespierre, Marx, Lenin, Hitler, and Mao.[8]

This type of "social doctrine" or "social theory" is frightening and has produced its fruit in the bloodiest of revolutions, such as that of France, Cambodia, Russia, and Korea.[9] In this type of thinking, the end justifies the means. The existing society and morals must be taken apart at any cost, and any means may be used to do so. Marxist revolutions find their beginnings in just such thought. Without the governance of God, the ultimate Lawgiver and Creator, the world unravels into tyranny and mass murder.

ROUSSEAU'S "RADICAL ETHICAL RELATIVISM"

Mix Rousseau's philosophy with Darwinism and humanism, throw in some communist ideologies, and you get a "radical ethical relativism" that is a potent cocktail in revolutionary thought and practice. Rousseau is considered by some to be the first writer to attack the institution of private property and thus a forerunner of communist thought. According to Rousseau, the state had the responsibility over the will of the majority to see that justice, equality, and freedom for all were obtained regardless of the measures required to reach their "ideal."

Rousseau's writing affected the thinking of men such as Hitler in the way he looked at those he considered "unfit" for his perfect Aryan world. There is an element in Rousseau's writings on education that implies only healthy children should be taught as opposed to what he termed the "useless cripple." His philosophy helped shape the thinking of the government of Nazi Germany and their "T-4" program to euthanize those they deemed unworthy in society. It was only the next logical step in eugenics, a concept widely accepted even by great "moral" leaders such as Theodore Roosevelt and Winston Churchill.[10] It shows how scary the mix of Rousseau's ideologies, Darwinism, humanism, and politicized science can be—much the same mix that is blinding people to the evil and holocaust that abortion is today.

Of course, this can only happen when the moral governance of God—the Creator who gives and values life in whatever form it may take—is ignored and forgotten. To God, there is not one child alive on planet earth today who is deemed "unworthy." God the Father loves every single one and has a special purpose for all of their lives. It is so like the devil to try to kill them and stop them from being the blessing to the world God intended them to be.

As I am writing this section I am thinking of my own niece, Reese Marie Rieth Miller, my sister and brother-in-law's daughter. Doctors diagnosed her at birth as being on the autism spectrum and hardly functional. After prayer and therapy, however, she became highly functional, is speaking, and was able to go to school by herself and make straight As. Reese now lives in Minnesota, where she has been mainstreamed into a regular classroom. We know what Nazi Germany would have wanted to do with her life, but this is not the morality of our nation.

ABRAHAM KUYPER: THE DUTCH STANDARD

The French Revolution—carried out with Rousseauian values—was bloody, left the nation shattered, and would infect Europe like the Black Plague well into the nineteenth century. A revolution without God is a frightening thing indeed. However, God had already prepared a man in Holland named Abraham Kuyper for the next century to be a forerunner of righteousness against this bastion of revolution.

To the American mind, revolution is a good thing. However, right after the French Revolution, the need in Europe was for anti-revolutionaries, or those who opposed the values introduced by Rousseau. It is comforting to see how in the midst of chaos and uncertainty, God always raises up His standard when the enemy comes in like a flood (see Isa. 59:19), and in Kuyper's case, *The Standard* was literal.

Abraham Kuyper (1837–1920) was a Calvinist and a minister of the Reformed Church. In every sense he was just that—a preacher of reform and a prophetic voice in his generation. In order to protect the faith and culture of his people, he courageously spoke out against the thinking introduced through Rousseau and the French Revolution that was threatening everything it touched. Unlike others whom God used as a voice from the pulpit, the Holy Spirit led Kuyper to engage in societal transformation through a variety of reformational practices.

For one, he started a newspaper in 1872 called *De Standaard* (Dutch for *The Standard*). His motto to rally his troops was "Fight the good fight of faith," which he used from his public pulpit for almost fifty years. *The Standard* was Kuyper's instrument to shape public opinion. He did this through writing editorials that established public debate, which could take place in the press as well as in Parliament. It also became his tool to express the party platform for the Anti-Revolutionary Party (ARP) that he formed. The ARP became the voice of righteousness and drew a line in the sand to protect Holland from suffering the same violent, godless revolution as France had.

Abraham Kuyper was deeply affected by his hero John Calvin, who as a young reformer helped build a government in the city of Geneva, Switzerland. By age twenty-five, Calvin had already been put in prison briefly after meeting with his cousin Robert Olivetan and Jacques Lefevre, who were Bible translators.[11] During his career, Calvin helped draft a constitution for the city. While he never held public office, he helped reform the infrastructure and economics of the city. Social structures such as hospitals, sewage systems, and education for all classes were established. He arranged that every family in the city would be visited by a minister once a year, in addition to the sick and poor being attended to regularly and everyone in the hospital visited.[12]

While this theistic society did not last because of the shortcomings in how it was executed (I definitely do not endorse all of Calvin's methods), it was still light years ahead of its time in thinking and practice.

THE NEED FOR GODLY JOURNALISM

Particularly at election times, *The Standard* was packed with short editorials or "leaders," urging, warning, and encouraging the party

157

faithful in the various electoral districts to stay the course and hold to their convictions. Kuyper's Bildungsdrang (Dutch for "desire for education") became an inner drive to turn his followers into competent citizens in a political system within which, before his time, they had not played a part.[13]

I believe that if we are to see righteousness and justice marry in the thinking and hearts of the nations, then we must see journalists write and newspapers print reformational platforms to be read by the general public. There are probably conservative newspapers today, but they are few and far between. The newspapers I know of are so infected by anti-Christian sentiments that they are just propaganda machines against God's kingdom. We need those who are called as newspaper publishers to publish the good news!

All in all, Kuyper, in my opinion, was an apostle for his time. In fact, he later established a university and eventually became prime minister. He is still a voice who speaks to us today through his 1898 "Stone Lectures at Princeton" that remind us that it was not the philosophers of the French Revolution who first introduced the idea that general populations had the right to be free. This idea "was not fished out of the unholy waters of the French Revolution, but stolen by the Rousseaus and the Montesquieus from the martyr's crown of the Huguenots."[14]

DRAWING A LINE IN THE SAND

Through the generations, we see those like Kuyper who have drawn a "line in the sand" against unrighteousness, but in order to really understand where our world is today and know what needs to be fixed in order to put the government on the shoulders of the Prince of Peace (see Isa. 9:6-7), there are two other ideologies we need to look at—utopianism and communism. You might ask yourself, "What does either of these have to do with me?" The people in czarist

Russia might have wondered the same thing before the Communist Revolution in 1917.

Just as God has a plan for this earth, the enemy of the kingdom of God does as well. He works to rearrange ideological structures in nations and continents to get God out of society and his evil plans into society. There is an interesting Scripture that speaks about this:

> *He shall speak pompous words against the Most High, shall persecute* [some translations say "wear out"] *the saints of the Most High, and shall intend to change times and law* (Daniel 7:25).

Satan wants to destroy us through lack of knowledge (see Hos. 4:6). He doesn't want anyone to know of his overarching scheme to rearrange governmental structures so he can establish his "kingdom on earth." Complacency and ignorance are two of his biggest tools! That is why I am writing about Rousseau, utopianism, and the like—to stir you up, equip you, and send you out into society as reformers in the Matthew 6:10, will-of-God-on-earth-as-it-is-in-heaven sense.

So it is important that we understand these two ideologies as we learn how to pray and act to change our nations.

Utopianism

Utopianism is the belief that man is inherently good and that given the right conditions good will emerge in a way that produces a perfect society. This theme is humanistic at its core and was one of the foundational premises of the so-called Age of Enlightenment.

It would follow then that since man is not sinful, there are only certain structures that need to be put in place for society to be perfect—for poverty to be eliminated, for disease to be practically put on hold, for social services to be provided efficiently, etc. Again, this is based on Rousseau's philosophies of humanity's natural goodness and government's role to purport its "good" upon the people as it deems necessary.

Again, this simply doesn't work because we as humans are sinners at heart. This is why we need a Savior and a book of laws written by the Creator to guide us in our societies.

Karl Marx and Communism

Communism, at its core, is utopianism. Karl Marx and Friedrich Engels thought they could create heaven on earth through their Communist Manifesto. They were revolutionaries who believed that any means to the end of achieving a communist state were right and good. They could have been the originators of the phrase "the ends justify the means."

Karl Marx was a German, born of Jewish parents. He had initially thought about becoming a Lutheran clergyman and even attended school to prepare for the ministry. He ended up studying law in Paris, where he met Engels. They believed that a utopia of the new communist man would emerge as an answer to all ills and that one day every nation would be communist.

The Communist Manifesto was written in 1848 in London, where Marx is buried. It called for the dissolving of the "bourgeoisie" in favor of the "proletarians," or working-class people. At the heart of this governmental philosophy is the abolition of private property as well as the family; all home education was to cease in favor of social indoctrination. The ideas of family, marriage, and God would be totally done away with in favor of free love. Communism was atheistic to the core!

Nikolai Lenin took up the cause in Russia, and an estimated sixty million people died as a result of the influence of communist ideologies. Tens of thousands of churches were torn down or desecrated. Solzhenitsyn sums up the reason for these fearful developments: "Men have forgotten God."[15]

Despite the fall of the USSR, communism is still very active around the world today. While it has failed in many nations, it is still very much alive in Latin America, China, North Korea, and other nations.

WANTED: REFORMERS!

God is still looking for Abraham Kuypers and William Willberforces. The church, the marketplace, and government leaders must forge alliances to stem the tide of godlessness and evil and shift our nations back to holiness and biblical alignment.

I am convinced that the people of God must look around and recognize those who are called as reformers to run for public office and be policy setters. We need to ask ourselves, "Where are the Wilberforces of today?" and, more poignantly, "Am I willing to become one?"[16]

Chapter Eight

REVERSING THE GENESIS CURSE: BIBLICAL ECONOMICS

THE GLASS CASE gleamed in the dusky light. I stared at the old worn garment of St. Francis of Assisi as I stood in a church in Florence, Italy. I searched my memory to recall what I knew of his life. "He changed the face of the church across the world," I mused, "with his sacrificial giving. He fought against corruption and excess as well." Then I had a stunning revelation. In the midst of all the good things that he did, such as giving up all his personal wealth (even to stripping himself completely of all his worldly belongings—right down to the garment on his back!), something else entered the mindset of the church through his teachings: the equation of poverty with spirituality. (In other words, the more spiritual you are, the less money you will have at your disposal.)

While St. Francis did some great things, we have carried this part of his mission too far into what has become a spiritual formula in the church today. We have come to believe that having wealth is wrong, when in fact it is how you obtain it and what you do with it that makes it righteous or unrighteous. As a result, the pervasive financial worldview in many churches today is: poverty equates spirituality, and therefore wealth is sinful.

I remember this affected my family, not because we believed that way but because the members of our church did. Therefore, they paid my pastor daddy a small salary and even criticized him so much when he bought a slightly nice used car that he ended up selling it. We were poor. In the United States some congregations would teasingly say about their pastors: "We keep them poor, and God keeps them humble."

What happened to us felt more like humiliation than humility, and it certainly didn't feel spiritual! I forgive them, God! (Maybe there are some other pastors or pastors' children who would like to join me in that prayer?)

BREAKING OLD MINDSETS

I realize now that we were victims of the mindset that poverty equals spirituality because our church members had somehow inherited that cultural bias. However, the Word of God says that it is the love of money (see 1 Tim. 6:10) that is sinful, not being the steward of wealth (see 1 Tim. 6:17-19).

Unless we change our worldview on money to a biblical stance, we will never be able to properly steward the earth. It takes wealth and influence to do that as a Holy Nation establishing His kingdom and His will on the earth—not only individually but collectively.

To truly understand how we should view wealth, we need to go all the way back to the garden of Eden. We need to realize that it was God's original plan to put us in the garden to steward it. At the time, it wasn't hard to take care of the garden. However, after Adam and Eve's fall, all of humanity was exiled from that perfect way of life. But our role in the earth never changed—we are still called to steward it, although now we have to deal with land that is cursed because of sin. In other words, we still have the same biblical mandate as Adam and Eve had. We are called to bring the earth back to its original state of productivity. The earth is cursed, but the curse can be reversed through understanding our covenant with God. Again, this call is stated in Matthew 6:10:

> *Your kingdom come. Your will be done on earth as it is in heaven.*

What is the curse that we need to reverse? It's found in Genesis 3:17-19:

> *Cursed is the ground for your sake; in toil you shall eat of it all the days of your life. Both thorns and thistles it shall bring forth for you, and you shall eat the herb of the field.*
>
> *In the sweat of your face you shall eat bread till you return to the ground, for out of it you were taken; for dust you are, and to dust you shall return.*

(I must admit that I have thought about this curse while diligently pulling weeds in my garden. I wonder if roses had thorns before the curse? I just noticed I have one in my finger from pruning my roses!)

These two Scriptures lead us to our role as Reformation Intercessors that I will address and explain in the next chapter. It is good to know that there are ways to pray to redeem the earth from this curse.

SCARCITY: THE EFFECTS OF THE CURSE

This curse produced something that is a basic principle governing the study of economics today—scarcity. According to Dictionary.com, *scarcity* means "insufficiency or shortness of supply, dearth."

When Jesus came to reverse the curse of the fall, He not only paid the price for our sin but, according to Galatians 3:13-14, broke the curse and its effects—scarcity, want, and lack.

> *Christ has redeemed us from the curse of the law, having become a curse for us (for it is written, "Cursed is everyone who hangs on a tree"), that the blessing of Abraham might come upon the Gentiles in Christ Jesus, that we might receive the promise of the Spirit through faith.*

Through the cross, we were grafted into the vine and receive the same blessings—or cursings—of which Israel was given the choice in Deuteronomy 28.

Again, remember that God so loved the world that He gave His Son to save the world as well as individual lives (see John 3:16). He loves all of creation! The earth, the sky, the invisible realm, all His created creatures, and especially His crowning creation—humanity. He wants to return us to the Genesis 1:28 mandate He gave us to fill, multiply, subdue, and have dominion over the earth.

> *God said to them, "Be fruitful and multiply; fill the earth and subdue it; have dominion over the fish of the sea, over the birds of the air, and over every living thing that moves on the earth."*

In other words, God never changed his mind—we have the same mandate Adam and Eve had. According to Genesis 1:28, we should do these things as stewards of the earth:

1. Be fruitful and multiply: "to be or grow great...to make large, enlarge, increase"[1]
2. Fill the earth: "to fill, be full...to consecrate"[2]

3. Subdue: "to subject, subdue...make subservient;"[3] "bring into bondage"[4]

4. Have dominion: "rule, subjugate"[5]

After looking at that passage in the original context, can we honestly say that we have done what we have been commanded to do?

It is also important to ask ourselves one other interesting question: Why did God command Adam and Eve to do those things in a perfect world? I believe it is because He knew that sin was going to come into all this perfection and human beings needed instructions on what to do after that happened.

According to the commentary in *Nelson's NKJV Study Bible*:

> The word subdue means "to bring into bondage," a military term used in the conquest of enemies. (Zechariah 9:15)
>
> As a king sets off to war to conquer a territory, so humans are told by the Great King to subdue the earth and rule it. Why this great need?
>
> The earth left to itself would not remain good. It would need us to "act as managers" who have the authority to run everything as God planned. This command applies equally to male and female.[6]

This makes even greater sense in the context of Colossians 1:19-20, in which God states that all things were reconciled by Jesus' sacrifice on the cross, whether things on earth or things in heaven.

HOW DO I REVERSE THE CURSE?

About this point, you might still be asking, "All right, Cindy, what does this have to do with me?" If you are a born-again believer, through becoming a follower of Christ you have been restored to the original mandate given in the garden. You are called to see His kingdom come and His will be done on the earth. This involves every structure of society, the thinking of individuals in nations down to the smallest child, every law, every government official elected according to a biblical design, and every economic structure according to God's blueprint—the Holy Spirit-inspired Word of God. In other words, you have the power and anointing to be a change agent to reverse the curse of scarcity, poverty, lack, corruption, humanism, disease, and any other thing that has resulted from the curse. It won't be perfect again until Jesus returns because sin still happens every day, but we must be stewards until then, taking care of all things according to the power God has put into each of us who are in Christ.

This is an absolutely amazing calling! It begins with a mother at home raising her children, the education of those little ones, all the way to the training of the generations in every sector of society. We must learn not only to read God's Word but read God's world in the light of His Word. God's Word gives us an X-ray view of what needs to be corrected and maintained in the earth.

When we lived in Colorado Springs, Colorado, my husband, Mike (who, by the way, has most of the brains in the family), began to teach on alternative economic systems. An alternative economic system is one based on something other than paper money, or the fiat system (a system whereby some sort of "note" or object is used to represent value and is backed by a government or a bank, even though the representative artifact—paper money, for example—has no inherent worth of its own). This is in contrast to a system based on a real commodity such as gold, silver, grain, or diamonds. His teachings led me to explore the Bible—the Manufacturer's handbook—to see what the Creator instituted in His economic structure.

While this is still in the formative state with me, there are basics that can be established.

Our term *economics* comes from the Greek word *oikonomia* or "stewardship of the house."[7] It is, in essence, the science of managing things that are in limited supply or can grow scarce. According to Tom Rose's book on biblical economics, scarcity for economists is a given they must deal with. Considering this, he poses the question:

> Can the existence of spiritual insight on the one hand, and the lack of it on the other, cause economists with the same professional training to arrive at opposing policy recommendations?[8]

Of course, we know the answer is yes. We as Christians also know that scarcity began with the curse of poverty that was released by the fall. However, Jesus paid the price to redeem us from the fall, and so we have been delivered from the curse of scarcity into abundance. Abundance is the antonym (or opposite) of scarcity. Thus we live according to a new principle in Christ:

Everything in our lives and the society we represent should produce increasing abundance.

We are called to be fruitful, told that "everything around us will multiply"; we are anointed to subdue and have dominion over anything around us. This is what it means to inherit the blessings of Abraham. We have been delivered out of lack and into abundance—out of the land of scraping to get by and into the land of God's abundance, a place where we will always have more than enough.

CREATOR-INSPIRED ECONOMICS[9]

Scarcity is not a mindset of all economists. It is the mindset of the liberal Keynesian economists who are the main advisors to the political left.[10] This comes along with the mindset that we live in a finite world where "what you see is all there is." If we are all a cosmic accident, we must control what little we have, as there is no way to get more.

Thus, all liberal economics focuses on government control and intervention as well as viewing the world through a lens of scarcity. For example, the late 1960s concern that the earth was getting overpopulated (Paul Ehrlich's book *The Population Bomb* greatly influenced this concern, much like the threat of "global warming" worries us today). This scarcity mindset focused on the earth's inability to support much beyond the earth's population at that time (which was somewhere around 3.5 billion people). Issues surrounding overpopulation became a major plank in the liberal economic mindset. Thus it is essentially your "patriotic duty" to reduce and/or control the population of the earth (hence abortion and birth control, China's one-child policy, etc.). That's the opposite of God's command to "be fruitful and multiply" (Gen. 1:28).

Obviously, as the world approaches seven billion people, we know that this is a completely fallacious argument. I've always said, "I'd challenge anyone to drive from Dallas to Amarillo and tell me that the earth is overpopulated." Statistically speaking, you could give every family on the face of the earth a half-acre of land, and all of them could be contained inside the continent of North America (with more than four million square miles left over), leaving the entire rest of the world to provide our natural resources, food, etc.

New schools of economics, such as supply-side and free-market economics, basically function from a prosperity mentality and are much more biblical in their worldview. They focus on growth and prosperity, not on scarcity and limitations. Free-market economics says just leave people alone and they will naturally do what is in their own self-interest to grow the economy, just as water flows downhill. Prosperity will then affect all who are willing to work for it—much different from the philosophy of taxing the rich to pay for government programs and welfare.

Stewardship is a very different concept than managing scarcity. Just look at how Joseph handled Potiphar's affairs, the prison he was thrown into, and then the nation of Egypt during famine (see Gen. 39–45). While all of the Middle East was starving, Joseph was using abundance to buy up everything that could be bought—he was not limited by the drought or unproductive lands!

In many ways these "abundance" schools of thought are much more in keeping with our roots. Free-market economics were widely accepted prior to the advent of socialism (for example, Adam Smith's "invisible hand"), but when the humanistic viewpoint began to take over our educational systems, the humanistic economic theories of Keynes took over economic thought as well. Since the late 1970s, Keynesianism has steadily been losing the war, but there is still a preponderance of this kind of thinking among members of the media, liberal politicians, and much of academia.

LIVING WITH AN ABUNDANCE MENTALITY

Abundance is God's desire for us. Why else would Jesus say that the thief comes to steal, kill, and destroy, but that He came *"that they may have life, and that they may have it more abundantly"* (John 10:10)? There are days when things are happening around me, and I know that the thief is trying to steal from me, my ministry, or our team at Generals International, and I will say out loud, "This is not

171

God's will for my life (or my family or ministry team)! I am called to have an abundant life. A life of abundance and not scarcity."

We put John 10:10 on the prayer board at the office and quote this over the ministry and staff each time we pray. Abundance is ours. It is a covenant right. The blessings of Abraham are ours because we have been grafted into God's family line through Christ Jesus (see Rom. 11). Therefore, our covenant rights give us the authority to break the Genesis curse of scarcity and lack. Deuteronomy 8:6-9 says:

> *Therefore you shall keep the commandments of the Lord your God, to walk in His ways and to fear Him. For the Lord your God is bringing you into a good land, a land of brooks of water, of fountains and springs, that flow out of valleys and hills; a land of wheat and barley, of vines and fig trees and pomegranates, a land of olive oil and honey; a land in which you will eat bread without scarcity, in which you will lack nothing.*

This means that one of those things that we have authority over in our societies is poverty. Believe it or not, it is entirely possible for God to give His children a plan to eradicate systemic poverty, or as I would define it:

Poverty that is completely through a society. A society's system of operation from the micro worldview of its people to the macro of the nation (i.e., culture, economic system) that releases poverty and not abundance for its citizens.

This, of course, is a huge job. It can only be done supernaturally. My suggestion is that we begin with the church at present. What do God's economic policies look like at both the local congregation level and the Holy Nation level? It is not enough to simply pray, *Let your kingdom come, your will be done on earth as it is in heaven*; we need to implement it. This takes a reformation of our thinking, and this is why this book is a reformation manifesto.

One of the major points that I wish to make in this chapter is that we are to put into place an economic system for the house of God. We need to learn how to develop a biblical philosophy of economics—or *oikonomia*—for our house and nation. This is part of being stewards of the earth!

Another reason it is so important for us to care about the poor and breaking the curse of poverty on our nations is that this was the subject of Jesus' first public sermon in the synagogue, where He read from Isaiah 61:1:

> *The Spirit of the Lord God is upon Me, because the Lord has anointed Me to preach good tidings to the poor.*

As a first step to this, each local congregation should ask God for a system to eliminate poverty for their members. Imagine a Sunday morning where the majority of the people attending have been able not only to pay their own bills but have money to share with others who are getting out from under the curse of poverty!

I am excited to say that our church, Trinity Church of Cedar Hill, Texas, has a plan to be a "poverty-free zone." One can take classes on how to get out of poverty. People bring money to the altar to give to others to help pay off their credit cards. They purchased a house for a widow whose husband and son died. People are giving goods from their stores to help the poor live a dignified life as well as giving cars so people can go to work. What has this done for the local church itself? As people get out of credit card debt, they have money to give to missions and other church projects.

Before we go any further in this chapter, let me give you some pointers to make sure that you are personally free from the curse of poverty:

1. Repent of any corrupt practices. Ask the Holy Spirit to reveal to you any sin that is hidden from your feeling of conviction, such as lying, not paying your bills, not paying your taxes, breaking any laws, charging interest to the poor, etc. Read the list of curses in Deuteronomy 28, and make sure that you have not participated in idolatry or any other sin that leads to these curses being visited upon your life.

2. Break the curse of poverty in the Name of Jesus.

3. Renew your thinking through a study of God's Word concerning your economic covenant rights as a child of God.

4. Pray to receive your covenant rights as a believer concerning the blessing of Abraham—wealth, prosperity, being the head and not the tail in society. (See Deuteronomy 8; Deuteronomy 28:1-14.)

This means that we have appropriated and understood God's plan in Deuteronomy to eliminate poverty:

Now it shall come to pass, if you diligently obey the voice of the Lord your God, to observe carefully all His commandments which I command you today, that the Lord your God will set you high above all nations of the earth. And all these blessings shall come upon you and overtake you, because you obey the voice of the Lord your God:

Blessed shall you be in the city, and blessed shall you be in the country.

Blessed shall be the fruit of your body, the produce of your ground and the increase of your herds, the increase of your cattle and the offspring of your flocks.

Blessed shall be your basket and your kneading bowl.

Blessed shall you be when you come in, and blessed shall you be when you go out.

The Lord will cause your enemies who rise against you to be defeated before your face; they shall come out against you one way and flee before you seven ways.

The Lord will command the blessing on you in your storehouses and in all to which you set your hand, and He will bless you in the land which the Lord your God is giving you.

The Lord will establish you as a holy people to Himself, just as He has sworn to you, if you keep the commandments of the Lord your God and walk in His ways. Then all peoples of the earth shall see that you are called by the name of the Lord, and they shall be afraid of you. And the Lord will grant you plenty of goods, in the fruit of your body, in the increase of your livestock, and in the produce of your ground, in the land of which the Lord swore to your fathers to give you. The Lord will open to you His good treasure, the heavens, to give the rain to your land in its season, and to bless all the work of your hand. You shall lend to many nations, but you shall not borrow. And the Lord will make you the head and not the tail; you shall be above only, and not be beneath, if you heed the commandments of the Lord your God, which I command you today, and are careful to observe them. So you shall not turn aside from any of the words which I command you this day, to the right or the left, to go after other gods to serve them (Deuteronomy 28:1-14).

These steps go along with the biblical promise that all of God's children—not just a few, the children of Abraham—have the power to get wealth!

And you shall remember the Lord your God, for it is He who gives you power to get wealth, that He may establish His covenant which He swore to your fathers, as it is this day (Deuteronomy 8:18).

What does this all mean to us? If we walk in God's plan for our lives, obey Him, and cause our nations to obey Him, God will give us such wisdom in business and finance that it would be an exception to have poverty in our midst rather than the rule. This is the opposite of the current economics based on scarcity—it is one based on abundance.

As I am writing this, I am thinking of being poor. We weren't dirt poor when I grew up, but we definitely had to struggle to pay our bills. I don't want anyone to have to go through that. I am thinking of the homeless people whom I have seen on the street corners of cities around the world. I want to help them, and I want us, the body of Christ, to pray and ask God to give us the answers to help them too. After all, we are commanded not to harden our hearts toward the poor.

If there is among you a poor man of your brethren, within any of the gates in your land which the Lord your God is giving you, you shall not harden your heart nor shut your hand from your poor brother, but you shall open your hand wide to him and willingly lend him sufficient for his need, whatever he needs (Deuteronomy 15:7-8).

This same chapter says we should be free from debt. I have read this over and over and thought, *"How can we implement this in our society today?"*

KICKING CORRUPTION OUT OF OUR NATIONS

The first and most basic principle to ending systemic poverty is to eliminate corruption from the church, and then the nation. Here is the bottom line:

> **We can never eliminate systemic poverty without eliminating systemic corruption.**

As one looks at healing economic systems, there must be a renewal of the minds of individual believers as well as congregations concerning ethics, honesty, and godly behavior in society. Corruption is a sin and must be looked upon as such. Yet when we accept it without even thinking about it—like those pastors I told you of earlier who weren't paying their taxes—how do we expect God to bless our casual unrighteousness?

This strikes at the heart of the matter. Judgment must begin at the house of God (see 1 Pet. 4:17). We cannot overthrow problems in nations that exist among ourselves. The Bible is clear about economic corruption in numerous passages. In fact, it is so anti-biblical to be corrupt that the Bible has clear "laws of restitution" that were to be paid by the penitent sinner who had stolen from others through corrupt practices.

Remember that Zacchaeus told Jesus he would pay half of his goods to the poor and if he had taken anything from anyone by false accusation, he would restore it fourfold (see Luke 19:8). Zacchaeus knew about restitution.

Legal restitution was 20 percent in addition to what you had taken (see Lev. 5:16; Num. 5:7). Being deeply repentant, Zacchaeus offered to go way beyond what was legally required.

Jesus must have used this story as an illustration to His disciples and a jumping off point to teach on the stewardship of "doing business until He returned," as He taught the parable of the minas at Zacchaeus' house (see Luke 19:1-27). Note that the reward for good business stewardship in this parable was to rule over cities. How can we transform cities if we cannot effectively deal with issues of poverty and corruption in the body of Christ?

Corruption leads to false dominion, where money is accumulated through greed. Corrupt leaders may become titans of the marketplace through a misuse of the money, influence, and power those bring, but they will never reform society. They are only in it for themselves, and their philanthropy is motivated by the tax advantages received from their giving.

GODLY GUIDANCE FOR LENDING TO THE POOR

Biblical economics has built-in safeguards to mitigate against corruption, especially in dealing with the poor and defending them from becoming the victims of usury. Usury is "the practice of lending money and charging the borrower interest, especially at an exorbitant or illegally high rate."[11] In fact, not only are we as believers not to participate in the practice of usury when we lend money, but we are not to charge poverty-stricken brothers and sisters in the Lord interest at all!

> *If you lend money to any of My people who are poor among you, you shall not be like a moneylender* [usurer—KJV] *to him; you shall not charge him interest* (Exodus 22:25).

Gary North gives a detailed explanation of this passage in his book *Honest Money*. He makes the point that we are not forbidden to lend and charge reasonable interest—in fact, the blessing of God upon a nation allows its people to lend to many nations and not borrow (see Deut. 28:12)—but we are forbidden to charge interest to the poor among us in the family of God.[12]

> *You shall not charge interest to your brother—interest on money or food or anything that is lent out at interest. To a foreigner you may charge interest, but to your brother you shall not charge interest, that the Lord your God may bless you in all to which you set your hand in the land which you are entering to possess* (Deuteronomy 23:19-20).

And this passage in Exodus says:

> *If you ever take your neighbor's garment as a pledge, you shall return it to him before the sun goes down. For that is his only covering, it is his garment for his skin. What will he sleep in? And it will be that when he cries to Me, I will hear, for I am gracious* (Exodus 22:26-27).

This section deals with both the lender's practices and the debtor's. The debtor cannot get multiple loans on the same collateral and then have any incentive to pay back the loan.[13]

God is very particular about how we treat the poor. Remember that one of the reasons the judgment of God came upon Sodom was because of how the city treated those who were destitute:

> *Look, this was the iniquity of your sister Sodom: She and her daughter had pride, fullness of food, and abundance of idleness; neither did she strengthen the hand of the poor and needy* (Ezekiel 16:49).

Part of the roll of Ezekiel as a prophet was to point out the unconscious sins of cities so that the people could repent. In this passage the Lord is dealing with the sins of Samaria as well as Sodom, but is also saying that Jerusalem's sins were much worse.

How Does My City Measure Up?

How do our cities measure up on God's plumb line? What do we do to eradicate systemic poverty? While the Scripture says that the poor will always be among us (see Mark 14:7; John 12:8), it is still our responsibility to see their need and find solutions (see Deut. 15:7-11).

Particularly, no born-again believer who is a regular tither and faithful member of a local congregation should have to stay on welfare (or the dole) on a long-term basis! Why?

Because their local congregation should have a plan in place to eradicate poverty among their membership! In fact, I am going to jump out into deep water here and state that I believe it is possible to see the kingdom of God so manifested in a nation that there is no need for a welfare system at all—especially for any believer! The church should be the solution provider for society. The governments of the earth should be able to look to us for answers to their problems with poverty.

I am aware that the thought of trying to develop structures to eradicate systemic poverty can be overwhelming, even at the level of our local congregations; however, the Word of God is clear that we are able to reverse the curse on any level. What we cannot do separately, we can do together.

Is Your Religion Pure?

The bottom line of all of this is the mandate that helping the widows and orphans among us is the purest form of following Christ's teachings:

Pure and undefiled religion before God and the Father is this: to visit orphans and widows in their trouble, and to keep oneself unspotted from the world (James 1:27).

The Creator has not run out of ideas or solutions, and there are people whom God has especially gifted with the ability to tap into supernatural intelligence to start the reversal of the Genesis curse. God will help us to "steward the house" by releasing His anointing to give supernatural solutions.

This will be done by those who have had their minds renewed through God and receive the calling of God to be economists. A mind anointed by God sees things through the belief that there is nothing impossible to God. A challenge is only an opportunity to see the power of God move in a supernatural way.

I mentor a group of women leaders who understand that world-view changes the way we see difficult situations and Satan's opposition. I told them one day, "Other people might see a serpent, but we see a handbag or even a pair of shoes!" Perspective! Israeli President Shimon Peres once said, "This year Israel will make out of [its] brains more than the Saudis will make out of their oil wells."[14]

Remember that we are to love God not only with our hearts and souls but with our minds (see Matt. 22:37). Through Christ we have supernatural thinking available to us. That is why it is so critical that we have our minds renewed on a daily basis through reading and studying God's Word. It is alive and powerful (see Heb. 4:12)!

The good news is that God hasn't stopped being able to anoint leaders, like Joseph in Egypt, who can receive divinely inspired economic plans. Those with this kind of Joseph gifting in business are able to hear God for a plan to eradicate poverty for their churches and cities. They need to realize that God has called them to this and begin to pursue Him with all of their hearts for answers. What is God speaking to your heart right now about this important topic?

KINGDOM BANKING

The Muslims have a system of banking. I know of churches who have established their own savings and loan companies and helped people with mircro-loans to start businesses. I am looking forward to more of this happening in the future.

While this is exciting, I believe that the establishment of Holy Nations and kingdom banks across the whole earth—all working together to see God's will being done just as it is in heaven—is the next necessary step we must take in biblical economics. I believe this is imperative because we will not be free to see the kingdom of God released in the nations of the earth without first having biblical *oikonomia*—stewardship of the house—and without such kingdom banks.

What do I mean by kingdom banking? Literally, the international development of a system of finance by and for the followers of Jesus Christ, committed to seeing God's kingdom come and His will done on earth as it is in heaven. This micro-level thinking is imperative if we are ever going to have the macro-level political and financial clout necessary to heal nations.

It is sad to think that we have not already done this. The Muslims are far ahead of us in their thinking. They already have banks set up based on Sharia law, and they have a system whereby they do not charge interest. In fact, when I was in England recently, someone gave me a copy of the Monday, April 23, 2007, issue of the *Financial Times*. This was the headline: "Britain First in West to Issue Islamic Bonds." The article proceeded to say:

> The move is unprecedented. Shari-ah compliant bonds
> have previously been issued by the governments of

Pakistan and Malaysia and also by corporate issuers around the world but never by a Western nation.

It also states that this is a move to underpin the City of London's financial role in encouraging Muslims there. It is a major step toward the Islamification of the United Kingdom—and its total control of the financial sector.

One of the most startling parts of the article stated that the total Islamic finance assets worldwide—including private equity and bonds—exceed 124.7 million pounds. That is approximately 249 million dollars!

My question is, "What is the amount of the Christian financial assets worldwide that we have as a Holy Nation—kingdom of God—financial system?" The answer: Absolutely none. No such system exists, as far as I know. In spite of all of our claiming that the wealth of the sinner is laid up for the righteous (see Prov. 13:22), we are far behind the kind of global thinking done by those in Islam.

All this makes me so sad that I feel like weeping. Yet there are globalists who are monetary scientists working totally outside of the box, pooling their funds to engineer financial changes worldwide. Doesn't this remind you of the Scripture passage in Luke 16:8, where the master commended the unjust steward:

> *For the sons of this world are more shrewd* [smarter in practical matters] *in their generation than the sons of light.*

CALLING ALL MODERN-DAY JOSEPHS AND DANIELS

The good news is that a new generation of Josephs, whom God has anointed to be monetary scientists, will connect with the

Daniels—God's political scientists—and work together to change the earth.[15]

If we are ever to take seriously our call to eradicate systemic poverty, then we need to understand that the God who is above all has all knowledge and wisdom and unlimited resources at His disposal. We are never going to be able to actually shift our thinking and the wealth needed to release God's will into the earth without new prayers for a new day. It is time now to delve into God's prayer strategies for our generation and begin to understand the necessity of becoming *Reformation Intercessors*.

Chapter Nine

LEGISLATING IN THE HEAVENS: REFORMATION INTERCESSION

THE AIR IN the room was electric. A group of dedicated leaders had come together in Washington, D.C. to "shift the nation." The Lord had shown us that we were to convene what amounted to a prayer court to intercede for the United States.

Just that day, Mike and I had taken a side trip to tour the Supreme Court building. As we walked up to the facility, we noted a little sign that read:

The court is in session. Please enter by the side door.

The fact that the court was in session that day was significant because we were about to pray some radical prayers that evening, which we believed would begin to turn the tide against unrighteousness in our nation. The date was June 22, 2006.

It is interesting how the Holy Spirit is in control of our lives, ordering our footsteps, even when we are not aware He is doing so. I often wonder, if one could peel back the veil between the visible and invisible worlds, if we would see the Lord's angels orchestrating

185

our movements. Personally, I believe we would. That thought is very, very comforting to me.

While taking a preliminary tour of that particular building the day before, I had stopped in the gift shop and picked up a gavel and block engraved with the words, *The Supreme Court of America*. At the time I thought, *What a great souvenir!* But the next day I knew that it was more than a souvenir. God wanted us to use it as a symbol of His judicial authority over the nations. We were to convene the court of heaven and legislate His will in the earth—and I would call that court to order using this gavel.

That night, as the meetings began, I felt we were to appeal to God as the great Judge of the universe concerning the unrighteous laws of our nation. I took the gavel and pounded it on the block, grabbing the attention of everyone in the room. Then I announced the vision that God had shown me: The Captain of the Lord of Hosts was waiting to come into the city with angels riding on chariots of fire. They were encircling the area and making way for His righteousness. (By the way, there was a war in the natural as well—the air conditioner was broken, and our skin glistened as we went into prayer and worship.)

During the time of worship, I stepped to the platform and began to prophesy: "I am going to wash Washington, says the Lord!" This "shifting of the nation" and our prayer assignments were set in motion through the prophetic words released that first night of the conference. The speakers were Dutch Sheets and Chuck Pierce. Dutch stood and shared that a prophet, Sam Brassfield, not knowing that Dutch was on a flight to Washington, D.C., had called his home to find him. He later connected with Dutch and gave him the word: "God says, I am going to wash Washington." Dutch went on to explain that he thought it was just a funny saying, until I got up and stated the same thing! Chuck Pierce, as he often does, tag-teamed as we flowed together in the Spirit and prophesied that the city was going to flood.

We asked Thomas, a youth leader who worked with Lou Engle and The Call movement, to pray and ask God to send His chariots of fire into the city to do war over unrighteous laws, such as those legalizing abortion. Thomas was himself almost a statistic on the list of aborted babies and prayed with great authority.

That night after the meeting, the skies over the Capitol looked like the bombing of Baghdad. Lightning and thunder rocked the skies, and rain began to fall. Over the weekend the rain increased, and the skies reflected what was going on in the spiritual, invisible realm, with angelic hosts fighting the powers of darkness over the city. There was a war going on in the heavenlies!

The news services on Monday, June 26, 2006 reported in the natural what the prophets had prophesied at our Shift the Nation conference. There was so much rain, one part of the city was flooded and a five-foot deep mudslide buried the Capital Beltway for one mile. This, we felt, was a sign that corruption was going to be exposed in D.C., and an Isaiah 35 "highway of holiness" movement would take place in the political system.

That is not all. Constitution Avenue flooded, as did the Justice Department and the Internal Revenue Department. Fish were found flopping in the streets from the deluge!

Part of our intercession was about the original design of the city by a Freemason named Pierre Charles L'Enfant. The metro-rail subway system at the L'Enfant stop was closed due to water on the electrical lines.

One final and significant sign happened in the days following our prayers. During these prayer times, I kept declaring that I saw the hand of God rocking a large tree back and forth and that it would be pulled up by its roots. A large elm tree—one of a pair that was located on the lawn of the White House—was uprooted during the storm and had to be replaced. (These two trees flank the White House in the picture on back of the twenty-dollar bill.) We saw this as another indication that hidden corruption would be exposed. (A second tree has since been planted.)

HIS KINGDOM COME

I am aware that the title of this chapter may sound strange to some readers. Allow me to explain legislating in the heavens.

God is the supreme ruler over the universe. He is the Lawgiver and wants His laws to be obeyed. Since that is so, we must ask ourselves some important questions like, "Why isn't His will being done on the earth?" and "What is my part in seeing His will—His kingdom laws—put into place in the earth (or in my family, city, or nation)?"

In a way, we can say we are called to see that God's law becomes the law in the land. I want to add here that this is not done through physical coercion, but as we pray, the hearts of the people turn to the Lord and they desire to put biblical laws in place. Our legislation begins in the heavens with prayer and is manifested in the earth through the changed hearts of people in authority. A portion of our God-given position as His sons and daughters is to be enforcers of His will. In *Possessing the Gates of the Enemy*, I described it this way:

> We are the enforcers of His will in the earth today as we use His name and pray His will through His Word. Human beings can now fulfill their God-ordained position given in the garden to subdue the earth and have dominion over it in the name of the risen Champion, Jesus Christ, while we at the same time discern and pray

for His will. Through our taking dominion over the works of Satan in the earth and praying in the name of our King, we establish His will on earth as it is in heaven. We, in the act of intercession, are His ambassadors plenipotentiary, fully empowered with full authority to pray on behalf of the mighty, awesome God of this universe.[1]

Our role in seeing God's will done on earth began in the garden. Going back to the premise that we are to "steward the house"—the earth—we need to understand our roles as intercessors in that Genesis mandate to *"be fruitful and multiply; fill the earth and subdue it;* [and] *have dominion"* (Gen. 1:28). Our stewardship not only includes things in the seen realm but also things in the unseen realm. In other words, we must take authority over the unseen (spiritual) realm that affects the seen (natural) realm. We have a saying here in the U.S.: "There is more to this than meets the eye," or there is more happening than we can see.

An important spiritual axiom in this regard is:

> **Stewardship of God's creation requires strategic, targeted intercession in order to see God's will done on earth as it is in heaven.**

This intercession must break down the demonic powers behind the ideological structures that influence people's thinking in areas such as humanism, poverty, and abortion.

There were things set in motion in the fall of Adam and Eve that need to be reversed through prayer. In order to steward all of creation, we must not only deal with what we see in the natural realm but also address the supernatural structures—called strongholds—that must

189

be broken in the heavenlies in order to see God's will done on the earth. Ephesians 6:12 makes this clear:

> For we are not wrestling with flesh and blood [contending only with physical opponents], but against the despotisms, against the powers, against [the master spirits who are] the world rulers of this present darkness, against the spirit forces of wickedness in the heavenly (supernatural) sphere (AMPC).

I call this kind of intercessory prayer legislating in the heavens. Let me explain: When the Congress of the United States meets—or Parliament in the United Kingdom, Australia, etc.—they legislate, or make laws. In legislating in the heavens, we decree through intercessory prayer that God's laws will be the laws of our nations. We also declare His will be manifested in every area of life and society.

Daniel 7:26-27 gives us a picture of this court of heaven:

> But the court shall be seated, and they shall take away his dominion, to consume and destroy it forever. Then the kingdom and dominion, and the greatness of the kingdoms under the whole heaven, shall be given to the people, the saints of the Most High. His kingdom is an everlasting kingdom, and all dominions shall serve and obey Him.

As intercessors of the Lamb, we serve as "assistant advocates" of the kingdom, charged with defending the King's people and prosecuting the King's enemies in the spirit realm (the adversary and his rebellious followers). Each time we come before the "bench" of the Judge of All, our Chief Advocate comes alongside and takes us by the arm to formally present us before the Judge and enumerate the legal credentials that He has delegated to us. We "practice before the bar" as lawyers sent from His high office—the Chief Intercessor and Chief Advocate of the redeemed.[2]

Our training as intercessors must include the presenting of a legal, biblical case before the throne of God. As we do this, the Holy Spirit begins to intervene in the affairs of men, laws, and nations to bring about the changes needed to establish His righteousness. In addition, the blessings of God will begin to pour out from heaven upon the nations of the earth because of that righteousness. This is why this kind of *reformation intercession* is so important. If we are to be reformers, we must reform the structures of the heavens as well as the earth because both are part of God's creation! There are dominions, or heavenly places, that hold whole sectors of society under their wicked sway and must be defeated through intercessory prayer.

A synonym for *dominion* is *kingdom*. Another way to think about our call as intercessors would be to paraphrase Matthew 6:10 this way: "Let your dominion come on earth, as it is in heaven."

Some nations are known as dominions, such as the Dominion of Canada. One of the Scriptures the founders chose as a cornerstone for our nation is Psalm 72:8:

> *He shall have dominion also from sea to sea, and from the River to the ends of the earth.*

I am aware that the term *dominion* has been given a bad name by those who have theologically abused it. However, I feel strongly that we cannot let this good biblical term be preempted because of wrong usage.

The Bible gives us sound doctrinal reason to take dominion over the powers of darkness and establish God's will—or dominion. We do this by prevailing against the powers of darkness and by reminding God of His laws and promises in Scripture. It is not that He has forgotten them, but He wants to see our faith in action as His legal representatives on the earth. He has given us authority here on earth and will not usurp that authority, but if we come to Him and ask that His promises be fulfilled and His laws enforced, then He will do just as He has written. There are several other passages that point to this doctrine of *reformation intercession*, such as Colossians 1:16:

> *For by Him all things were created that are in heaven and that are on earth, visible and invisible, whether thrones or dominions or principalities or powers. All things were created through Him and for Him.*

Since God created His order in heaven and earth, both in the visible and invisible realms, it stands to reason that when Satan began to set up his demonic, invisible structures he would counterfeit God's plan. Ephesians 1:20-23 gives us another biblical snapshot of heaven's authority over Satan's counterfeit systems:

> *Which He worked in Christ when He raised Him from the dead and seated Him at His right hand in the heavenly places, far above all principality and power and might and dominion, and every name that is named, not only in this age but also in that which is to come.*
>
> *And He put all things under His feet, and gave Him to be head over all things to the church, which is His body, the fullness of Him who fills all in all.*

Simply put, we must establish God's kingdom according to His divine rule in each sector of society by dethroning the powers of darkness that hold the nations in their grip.

Daniel described the invisible realm he saw in a vision when he exclaimed:

> *I watched till thrones were put in place, and the Ancient of Days was seated* (Daniel 7:9).[3]

There cannot be two ruling authorities over one geographical region. There will either be ruling powers of God or ruling powers of Satan. There is an ongoing battle for authority over a region that won't be finally settled until we intercede or Jesus returns and casts Satan and his minions into the lake of fire. We need to pray that God's kingdom authority will be established over our nations. Of course, regions will not be free once and for all from Satan's attacks until Jesus returns. Each generation needs to watch and pray over their own generation.

You might be thinking, "That sounds like a huge endeavor! How can I, one person, do such a thing? Isn't that scary or dangerous?" No, it isn't, but it does require courage and the knowledge of how to proceed in a biblical, non-presumptive manner.

EVERY PRAY-ER MATTERS

This is my reply to those people who are feeling overwhelmed at this and wonder where they fit into the scheme of things: You are important and strategic in some sector of society and culture. Each person who prays—each "pray-er"—is critically important to this task. There is a sphere of authority that you have that no one can touch like you can. You simply need to determine what that is and do the part that pertains to you. God will raise up thousands of others who will do their part, and the overall job will be done. This reminds me of the old adage: "How do you eat an elephant?" Answer: "One bite at a time."

You might also ask, "Well, why does it have to be me? Why doesn't God just take care of it? After all, isn't that His role and not mine, to take authority over wickedness?"

Again, going back to our role as enforcers, the answer is that the Lord has given into our hands the job of legislating His will in the earth. He has given us the authority and weapons to do this through what we call binding and loosing:

> *Assuredly, I say to you, whatever you bind on earth will be bound in heaven, and whatever you loose on earth will be loosed in heaven. Again I say to you that if two of you agree on earth concerning anything that they ask, it will be done for them by My Father in heaven* (Matthew 18:18-19).

Binding (or *deo* in the Greek, "to tie") and loosing (or *luo*) were used in legal terminology at the time of Christ. When the courts of His day would decide a case, they would either say, "We bind (or forbid)" or "We loose (or permit as legal) this in Israel." They would decide what was lawful or illegal, forbidden or allowed, in their nation using this same terminology.[4]

Note that Jesus did not say, "Ask Me to bind or loose." He said, "Whatever you bind or loose ("in My name" is a given here) on earth will be done." He said we are to do it in His name. Therefore, it stands to reason that if we do not take our place of authority in intercessory prayer, then wicked laws have every legal right to be put into place.

We need to pray and do. By this I mean we need to bind the powers of darkness that are blinding the eyes of those who make laws in our nations as well as become voices who speak out against sin in every sector of society.

Literally, Jesus told us that whatever we loose in prayer—or permit—will be legal in our nation, and whatever we bind—or declare illegal—in intercession will be illegal. This is the basis upon which we can "convene the court of heaven" through our intercessory prayers and legislate in the heavens certain laws of our nations. Dutch Sheets sums it up nicely in his book *Intercessory Prayer*:

> Although Jesus fully accomplished the task of breaking the authority of Satan and voiding his legal hold upon the human race, someone on earth must represent Him in that victory and enforce it.[5]

GETTING GOD'S PRAYER STRATEGY

How do we know what to bind and loose? God reveals His will in His Word. By studying the Bible, we know what does not line up with His will, and then we develop a prayer strategy to "legislate" His will, or bring our world into alignment with His Word.

When a general goes to war, he prepares a plan. In order to develop this plan he needs to know the topography of the land, where the battle will take place, the weapons the enemy has in their arsenal, and even the way the opposing general thinks. He does this through what is called gathering intelligence.

It is no different when we go to fight a spiritual battle against all the strategies that Satan has put in place against our nations. We must gather spiritual intelligence and a plan on how we will pray. My friend George Otis Jr., who created the excellent *Transformation* series, has coined the phrase for this type of plan development. He calls it *spiritual mapping*. Spiritual mapping gives us an X-ray of what is happening in the invisible realm so we know how to pray effectively.[6]

We must study the strongholds or illegal places of our nations and put together an intercessory plan to legislate God's will into every sector of society. For too long we have been ignorant of Satan's devices (see 2 Cor. 2:11).

How does one develop a spiritual map or prayer strategy for a specific sector of society? Here are some good questions to start with:

1. Who were the founders of your city?

2. What did they believe?

3. Were their beliefs biblically based?

4. How did their actions affect the society in which you live?

5. If the founders founded your city on righteous truth, when did this change and who changed it?

6. How has this affected the thinking of your society?

7. What does your society believe and teach through sectors such as education, media, and other channels of communication?

8. What strongholds have developed as a result of this wrong thinking, laws, or actions?

I am going to illustrate three areas as examples for prayer that need serious legislating in the heavens. They were chosen because of their particular influence on nations and their cultures. Each is a mind-molder in some way and key to renewing the hearts and worldviews of our nations.

Education

Let's put the above in the context of teaching nations, or education. This is how I would do this for the American education system, starting with answering the eight questions presented above:

1. The founders were godly believers who taught from righteous educational textbooks such as *The New England Primer.*

2. Their beliefs were that we should teach our children based on Scripture.

3. Their beliefs were biblically based.

4. As long as the original methods of education were in place, the nation and its children prospered.

5. Education took a turn away from God beginning in a visible way in 1933, with the Humanist Manifesto and the change in teaching philosophy presented through the "Father of Modern American Education," John Dewey.

6. Every sector of society has been influenced through humanist doctrine.

7. The educators in general have been educated through situation ethics, the nonethical approach that has led to a moral breakdown in our society.

8. Strongholds of humanism (remember, the humanist believes that the universe is self-existing and not created) have now permeated film, television, art, science, architecture, and all teaching of the liberal arts in universities.

How does one, on a practical level, begin to "demolish" the stronghold of humanism in our educational system?[7]

1. Be informed. Know what is being taught to students on every level in the schools in your area.

2. Obtain a roster of teachers, look at the curriculum being taught, and find out what the teaching philosophy of the school system is.

3. Go to the library and see what reading material is provided for students.

4. Find an interested group of Christian students and encourage them to form a prayer group on campus. Get as close as you can yourself to the campus and pray. Intercede for God to bring others across your path to join you in prayer.

5. Like Daniel, repent for the sins of the school that your children attend or that your tax money funds (see Dan. 9:8-15).

6. Ask God if you should fast. I suggest doing so.[8]

Make a list of the points on the Humanist Manifestos I, II, and III, and ask God to reverse these strategies that have been put in place in your schools. A few of these would be:

- The teaching of evolution
- The belief that God is not a prayer-hearing God
- The endorsement of sexual promiscuity

Last, but certainly not least, fast and pray for God to send a mighty revival among the students.

This is only a partial list. Be led of the Lord in your praying, and He will fill in the other specifics that pertain more directly to your area.

Architecture

While teaching in a church in Phoenix, Arizona, I shared about the Humanist Manifesto and the devastating spiritual results it has had in our school systems. During that time, I also had a revelation that the Lord would use the graduates of the various colleges, such as the school of music, architecture, etc., to go back on their campuses to pray and intercede for God to bring revival to those schools. Then, through their legislating the will of God in these schools, God would free the minds of the students to be open to learn biblical truth, even to hunger and search for it.

Having lived in Arizona as a child, I remembered that the famous architect Frank Lloyd Wright had lived in that area. In studying about his life, I found out that he believed in free love and that he felt he was "above normal social conventions." He had affairs while he was married and would travel between Wisconsin and Scottsdale, Arizona each year with a group of thirty or more students.

There is a saying, "From the roots grow the shoots." What is planted through a life affects the particular sphere that one influences. Wright's unholy roots affected the schools of architecture he founded. The "unholy" part needs to be repented of, so the good teaching of how to develop beautiful plans for buildings can be released.

In the Bible, Nimrod was a city builder who did so unrighteously. Israel needed to repent of his unrighteousness to get back into favor with God. We need to repent of past sins and pray that God will release righteousness into the teaching of architecture today.

The Entertainment Industry

There can be no doubt that this industry can be a major mind-molder for either good or evil. Media is, without a doubt, one of the most important influencers of culture around the world. Much prayer has gone on in Hollywood from groups such as the Hollywood Transformation Group. I have personally been involved in prayer gatherings at major Hollywood studios.

There has been a systematic plan by the homosexual community to infiltrate Hollywood. Here are some of the points of *The Homosexual Manifesto*:

> We shall write poems of the love between men; we shall
> stage plays in which man openly caresses man; we shall

make films about the love between heroic men which will replace the cheap, superficial, sentimental, insipid, juvenile, heterosexual infatuations presently dominating your cinema screens.[9]

In addition, it also states that all laws banning homosexual activity will be revoked. Their writers and artists have determined to make love between men fashionable, and could very well succeed because they are adept at setting styles. It also states that the family unit will be eliminated.

If you look at Hollywood and theater today, you will notice that almost all movies and plays will display at least one homosexual in some kind of positive light, often as the witty friend of straight friends. This has caused desensitization to homosexuality—exactly as planned.

While we never want violent acts to be performed against any member of society, we must be willing to stand up and say that the ideas presented in *The Homosexual Manifesto* are sinful and perverted. (See, for example, what Romans 1:24-27 has to say about homosexuality.)

It is sobering to say that there are nations today where pastors can be jailed if they openly speak out against homosexuality from the pulpit. However, we must be willing to do just that even if it means going to jail.

We need to intercede for Hollywood and the homosexual community because homosexuality has become intertwined with the arts on every level. The Lord wants to touch those who are stars in the eyes of the world so they will have a righteous influence. Intercession must be made on behalf of those in media and communication because what goes across the airways touches millions of people the world over. It affects what cultures and societies think, wear, act, and feel.

At one time the church had godly sway over the movie-making industry. There was even a production code that was strengthened and fortified by the Catholic Legion of Decency, which designated "indecent" films Catholics should boycott. Hollywood chose this instead of government censorship. It began as the Hays Code and was adopted in 1930 and abandoned in 1967 in favor of the Motion Pictures Producers and Distributors (MPAA) film rating.

The three "general principles" of the Hays Code were:

1. No picture shall be produced that will lower the moral standards of those who see it. Hence the sympathy of the audience should never be thrown to the side of crime, wrongdoing, evil, or sin.

2. Correct standards of life, subject only to the requirements of drama and entertainment, shall be presented.

3. Law, natural or human, shall be not ridiculed, nor shall sympathy be created for its violation.

Here are a few other specifics:

- Nudity and suggestive dances were prohibited.
- The ridicule of religion was forbidden, and ministers of religion were not to be represented as comic characters or villains.
- The depiction of illegal drug use was forbidden, as well as the use of liquor "when not required by the plot or for proper characterization."
- References to "sexual perversion" (such as homosexuality) and venereal disease were forbidden.

- "Scenes of passion" were not to be introduced when not essential to the plot.[10]

What happened to this system? First of all, the Christians no longer paid attention to the Legion of Decency and failed to boycott the movies that were rated "indecent." Filmmakers started going around them and found that they could still make money. The church lost its voice.

There cannot be a more critical area for intercessors to focus on in prayer than Hollywood and the media. We also need to intercede for the Christians who are working diligently to change this area of influence.

Many nations of the world have their own film industries, and there is a great need to spiritually map their roots and develop prayer strategies to take dominion in the heavenlies over these molders of society. We all want to see the will of God done on earth as it is in heaven, and targeting these areas is one way to see it happen.

It Is Up to Us

I believe God is raising up a powerful army of intercessors of all ages who will give their lives to pray for God to change the places where they live into holy habitations of peace, righteousness, and joy. Will you be one of them?

Chapter Ten

COSTLY GRACE

THE CONFLICT IN Dietrich Bonhoeffer's heart must have been wrenching as he boarded the plane back to Germany from the United States in July of 1939. All his life he had prepared himself as a theologian, spent his days studying the Scriptures, and loved God with all his heart.

It had only been one month prior that Dietrich had left his German homeland for America, planning not to return until after the war. What was he doing going back so soon? The Nazis had overtaken his nation and were destroying it with their false ideologies. I can only imagine the various conflicting words of counsel that must have passed through his mind and heart that day. He was just thirty-three years old, his whole life ahead of him.

A defining conviction thrust Dietrich toward his destiny as a voice for the salvation of his nation. He wrote to friend and fellow pastor Reinhold Niebuhr before leaving America,

> I shall have no right to participate in the reconstruction of Christian life in Germany after the war if I do not share the trials of this time with my people.... Christians

in Germany will face the terrible alternative of either willing the defeat of their nation in order that Christian civilization may survive or willing the victory of their nation and thereby destroying our civilization. I know which of these alternatives I must choose, but I cannot make this choice in security.[1]

Dietrich came from a long line of those who stood against the status quo for the sake of the kingdom of God. I believe God gives generational blessing and strength that produce a strong legacy for the Lord's purposes at moments of crisis. This was the case with Dietrich Bonhoeffer.

He had already taken to the radio airwaves, in 1933, to warn against the dangers of serving an immoral leader. He left the Lutheran Church and helped form the Confessing Church in response to the mainline churches' support of the Nazis. This church protested what they called the "Nazified Pulpit, Nazified Christian Life, and Nazified Clergy." A friend of Bonhoeffer, Eberhard Bethge, stated it this way:

> We did not interpret our decision as a choice between Christ and Hitler, between the cross and the swastika, and certainly not a decision between democracy and a totalitarian regime. Rather, we understood the issue as one between a biblical Christ and a Teutonic-heroic Christ, between the cross of the gospels and one formed by the swastika.[2]

Turning the Tide of Evil

A close group of friends and family stood with Dietrich against a seemingly impossible tide of evil coming against their nation. Deception as to the true intent of Hitler's policies and programs was rampant, and at that time the world both inside and outside of Germany felt that Hitler could not be stopped.

Being a Bible teacher, part of Bonhoeffer's resistance was to give instruction through God's Word—the truth that sets men and women free. He trained ministers at Finkenwalde. The Nazis declared the seminary illegal in 1937. No wonder Dietrich fled to America to use his gift. However, his catalytic decision to return home formulated from something deep in his heart—he wanted his nation to be free from tyranny.[3]

Less than a year before fleeing to America, he went to see the destruction of German synagogues and Jewish homes and businesses after Kristallnacht ("Night of Broken Glass"), November 9-10, 1938. It was a night of riots throughout Germany and in parts of Austria, attacking Jews, smashing their shop windows, and burning their holy places. Bonhoeffer went where the violence had been heaviest in Berlin in spite of being forbidden to go there by the Nazis. After this he worked tirelessly to smuggle Jews out of the country.

After his return from the U.S., Dietrich miraculously got a job as an agent in military intelligence. Through this he was able to travel and try to gain support for the cause to overthrow Hitler's regime. He was part of a botched plot to assassinate Hitler along with a number of other top Nazi officials.

Dietrich was arrested along with his sister Christel and her husband, Hans von Dohnanyi, on April 5, 1943, at the house of his parents. Eventually his brother Klaus and another sister's husband, Rudiger Schleicher, were arrested as well. At the time of his arrest, Dietrich was engaged to be married, so this must have been especially hard on his fiancée. As it turned out, they would never marry.

What Satan meant for evil, God turned for good, as Dietrich wrote some ten thousand pages while in prison. His letters were smuggled out through friends and guards. While I do not sub-scribe to all of his theological points, he's a powerful example of a reformer. While in prison he constantly cheered up fellow prisoners and ministered grace to all he came in contact with—even his jail-ers. He spent his last days on earth ministering comfort and com-munion to others.

In the end, Dietrich Bonhoeffer was sentenced to be hung. He was thirty-nine years old. Not only was he executed, but his brother Klaus and his sisters' husbands were as well—a huge blow to the whole family.

April 9, 1945, is a day that will be remembered as a clarion call to resist unrighteousness. That was the day Dietrich spoke to the wit-nesses of his execution, "This is the end for me, the beginning of life." The Allies liberated Flossenburg, the concentration camp that was his final place of imprisonment, only a few days after his death.

COSTLY GRACE

It has been said that the blood of the martyrs is the seed of the church. Bonhoeffer called what he believed in *costly grace*. In his own words: "Cheap grace is the deadly enemy of our Church. We are fighting to-day for costly grace."[4]

Let me be quick to say that I am not advocating salvation by any-thing but grace alone. However, since our grace cost Christ every-thing, we need to be willing to give Him everything for righteousness' sake. Following Christ is costly in terms of reputation, money, time, and how we live our lives. God looked down on the sin of the world and it grieved Him. So it should grieve us to see our society and nation bound with laws and actions that are sinful.

THE VISIBLE CHURCH

The role in which Bonhoeffer saw himself stemmed from his belief in the visible church as opposed to the church that has nothing to do with what is happening concerning the government and its actions. Historically in the United States, pastors have been very involved in the politics of our nation, even to the point of preaching "Election Day" sermons. Those who ran for office would come to church to hear what God and the Bible said about the current issues of the day. It was the role of the pastors to keep the nation on a biblical course.

During the American Revolution, pastors even stepped out from behind their pulpits to form what was known as the "Black Regiment." They were called this because of the black pastoral robes they wore at that time. Pastors actually led their congregations into battle against what they felt was the unrighteousness of the crown of England. One such pastor was Peter Muhlenberg.

Muhlenberg struggled with whether a pastor should be involved in politics. He then considered what the Bible says about there being a time for peace and a time for war (see Eccles. 3:1-11). After preaching a fiery message on that theme, he cried out, "It's time to fight for those freedoms that we hold so dear. It is time for war!"

I am sure there were gasps from the church members as he proceeded to take off his robe and stand before his congregation in the full uniform of an officer of the Continental militia. He marched to the back of the church, declaring to all, "If you do not choose to be involved, if you do not fight to protect your liberties, there will soon be no liberties to protect!"[5]

Just outside the church army drummers waited. At Pastor Muhlenberg's command, they began to beat out the call for recruits. God's conviction fell on the men of the congregation. One by one they rose from their pews and took their stand with the drummers.

Some three hundred men from the church joined their pastor that day to fight for liberty.

Today I believe God is raising up an army among the body of Christ that will stand up to the opposition against biblical truth in their nations. We need pastors and leaders who will "take off their clerical robes"—both in and out of the pulpit—and be a voice for righteousness in the land.

THE REBELLION OF DISBELIEF

Down through the ages there have been theologians who, rather than help to heal their nations, have hindered them through the tearing down of the validity of God's Word as the standard of truth. One such man was Julius Wellhausen. Before he came on the scene, there was little doubt in the minds of the general public that Scripture was the *inerrant*, absolute truth of God.

Wellhausen started a whole new line of thinking called higher criticism. In 1883 he published a book that taught that the first five books of the Old Testament were a combination of the work of many authors rather than Moses under divine inspiration. Up until that time the general thinking among believers—even nations—was that they could trust the Bible for answers on how to live their lives. This teaching cracked the bedrock of belief that God is the Creator and Ruler of the universe and as such deserves to be obeyed. To many the Bible became just another book. No longer considered divine revelation and God's law, it was a book of good ideas and historical moral writings.

In the sixteenth century, Luther's rallying cry, "The just shall live by faith," was a high point of Christianity in Germany, but Satan counterattacked with a triple-whammy: Wellhausen's higher criticism, Darwin's evolutionary theory, and Marxism. These struck a deep societal blow to the modern world. If the Bible could not be trusted as God's Word, as Wellhausen proposed, then maybe Darwin was right. If Darwin was right, then maybe there wasn't a God after all, and Marx was right that religion (i.e., Christianity) was merely "the opiate of the people."

Most of the universities, at least in America, that were founded to glorify God—such as Harvard, Princeton, and Yale—are now bastions of religious liberalism and secular humanism. I have visited campuses where the bells of the chapels that used to peal out an early morning call to prayer are now used for Buddhist meditation. The Old University of Chicago was founded as a place to train ministers and evangelists. Today the University of Chicago School of Divinity teaches world religions, and Christianity as just one among many of equal value.

THE GREAT DIVIDE

In America in the twentieth century, a great rift developed between liberalism and biblical truth. The liberals (who called themselves "modernists") went with Wellhausen, Darwin, and Marx, cobbling together a religious worldview that eventually denied the fundamentals of historic Christian faith. They wanted the ethics and social justice of Jesus, but they didn't want the doctrine of Christianity.

Meanwhile, evangelical conservatives (whom the liberals call "fundamentalists") held fast to the reformation cry, "The just shall live by faith," and took stand after stand for righteousness. However, liberals continued to insist on justice based on social conviction rather than righteousness. While most evangelicals still keep the light of Jesus Christ bright in the area of preaching salvation, many no longer see it as their Christian duty to extend that saving grace beyond the four walls of their church. For the most part they opted out of the civil rights movement, remained silent about domestic abuse, and rushed to the suburbs. This void has been filled by feminists founding battered women's clinics and homosexuals helping the poor. The "good deeds" of our cities are often done by groups that socially and politically stand against what the Word of God says. While I am grateful that people are helping, we believers should obey God's Word and be shining lights and, to our shame, have not always done so. On the other hand, many hospitals were started by believers and there is biblically based helping of the poor that is being done by the church.

LET THE CHILDREN COME

Perhaps one of the reasons the social service systems of the world are going bankrupt is that the church has given up her role in caring for the poor and needy. Here in the United States, we have a foster-care program for children from troubled families. At eighteen years of age, these kids are thrust out of the program and into the world. Often they live in as many as five or six homes over time, and many are abused in some manner. It is time the church gets involved in these kinds of programs.

Another area in which the church could help is adoption. On July 7, 2007, a Youth Prayer Day was held here in the United States called The Call Nashville. One of the speakers challenged people to be willing to adopt children who were born to mothers who are involved in drug abuse.

In response, a Caucasian couple came forward, carrying a beautiful African American/Caucasian four-year-old in their arms. They told the story of how they had had a baby who was stillborn at full term. They worked for a pro-life clinic at the time, and a young mother who decided against aborting her child gave her baby to them to raise. Having so recently lost her own baby, the adoptive mother still had milk and was able to nurse the baby as her own.

I believe this is a prophetic picture for our generation. God is giving us, His church, the chance to rescue some of the next generation waiting to be born through our willingness to open our homes and adopt children. With all my heart I know that God is going to require members of churches who think that they are beyond the point of raising a child to be willing to adopt children others planned to abort. We need to prove not only through our words but through our deeds that we are serious about marrying righteousness with justice in our land.

This kind of action is costly, but Jesus paid a costly price so that we could obtain grace. We need to seriously think about the message given to us through Christ's example: "Let the little children come to Me" (Matt. 19:14). We can actively make a difference in our culture. The Message says it like this:

> *So here's what I want you to do, God helping you: Take your everyday, ordinary life— your sleeping, eating, going-to-work, and walking-around life—and place it before God as an offering. Embracing what God does for you is the best thing you can do for him. Don't become so well-adjusted to your culture that you fit into it without even thinking. Instead, fix your attention on God. You'll be changed from the inside out. Readily recognize what he wants from you, and quickly respond to it. Unlike the culture around you, always dragging you down to its level of immaturity, God brings the best out of you, develops well-formed maturity in you* (Romans 12:1-2).

Here are some things you can do to make a difference:

1. Ask God whom you can personally help.
2. Don't be silent when things are wrong and you see God's laws broken in your culture.
3. The world will try to conform you to its pattern—don't let it!
4. Study God's Word diligently and regularly.

It is critical that we return to teaching the Word of God in every area of life. We are so influenced by our culture that some Christians don't see anything wrong with exchanging sexual partners. On the university campuses they call it "hooking up," and many times don't even know each other's names. There desperately needs to be teaching to break down the situation ethics that have permeated every part of our lives.

Rather than a social gospel without laws, we need to teach right from wrong and be willing to call sin—sin. Holiness needs to be the theme of the day so the fear of the Lord and the wisdom that comes with it will once again fall on our nations.

There are glimmers of hope all across our university campuses. One of the most exciting of these is the 24/7 movements springing up around the world where young people pray for the sick and release the miraculous on campus after campus. As of this writing, I know of at least sixty college and university campuses in America with 24/7 prayer taking place.

SUPERNATURAL BREAKTHROUGH

The supernatural breaks down all the natural arguments against God's existence. When you have a terminal illness and God completely heals you, you know that He is real. The power of God breaks down the stronghold of humanism every time. God's power trumps Satan's grip on culture like nothing else will do.

Jaeson Ma writes in his book *The Blueprint* of an encounter on the campus of the University of California, Los Angeles (UCLA) where a fraternity brother miraculously started walking without his crutches in front of a crowd of onlookers after a group of students prayed for him. Many were weeping at the sight. The healing presence of God was so strong; the people were in awe of God's power that manifested right on the school grounds.[6]

It is important to note here that part of discipling nations includes releasing the supernatural power of God. Remember that the commission that Jesus gave us before He ascended into heaven cannot be found solely in Matthew 28:19-20. The second half of our discipling mission comes through the empowerment given through the Holy Spirit's visitation at Pentecost. Look at how Mark completes the Great Commission in His gospel:

> *And He said to them, "Go into all the world and preach the gospel to every creature. He who believes and is baptized will be saved; but he who does not believe will be condemned. And these signs will follow those who believe: In My name they will cast out demons; they will speak with new tongues; they will take up serpents; and if they drink anything deadly, it will by no means hurt them; they will lay hands on the sick, and they will recover"* (Mark 16:15-18).

Signs and wonders bypass the humanist intellect and reveal God in a way nothing else will. When we pray for homosexuals dying with AIDS and they are healed, they will know that the God of the Bible is the real God. Even ardent atheists, when eaten up by cancer, are open to the idea of a loving Savior who can heal their bodies.

If we will only allow Him to lead us in prayer and pray as He instructs, miracles in businesses and schools across the nations will result in book-of-Acts-type evangelism. If we have nets readied for the harvest through our local congregations, this will result in an enormous multiplication of the kingdom.

My good friend Ed Silvoso points out that the church was added to and multiplied after Pentecost. This resulted in a whole city being filled with the message of Jesus Christ (see Acts 4:16). God literally gave us the power to disciple nations through supernatural means. Miracles provide us with a reformational witness of the truth that only Jesus is *"the way, the truth, and the life"* (John 14:6). We need to be much more proactive in taking miracles to the streets to change our cities for righteousness' sake.

As I mentioned before, in 1967 America experienced the "summer of love." People came to San Francisco from all over the world for free sex and drugs. A culture built on drugs was loosed by that generation. Psychedelic music was written under the influence of psychedelic drugs.

Around the same time in California, there was something called the Jesus Movement, when many were swept into the kingdom of God. Thousands were saved during that time. Young people were baptized in the ocean, and people like me were called "Jesus People" or "Jesus Freaks." Our motto was "Jesus is THE WAY." We loved God radically and passionately. However, somehow that move of God never really permeated society.

Today we are in the beginning stages of another Jesus movement with evangelism and miracles breaking out on college campuses. It is critical that we mix this fresh move of God with the reformation message and raise up a new generation of voices for righteousness. We desperately need a countercultural movement and holy revolution to break with postmodernism.

I want you to know that while writing this book, as I have typed out line after line, there has been a prayer in my heart:

> *Lord, use this book to raise up a new generation of reformers who are countercultural. Father God, we need a holy revolutionary people who will be salt and light in their communities and nations! O God, start a movement of holiness, using this book!*

I pray that message comes through these pages, not just from what I have written but from the working of the Holy Spirit, stirring your heart to be a change agent for the kingdom of God.

A NEW REFORMATION

Our times require a new reformation—not like the old one that called for the reform of the church only (although there are aspects of the church that still need to become "new wine"), but with societal reformation added to the mix.

Charles Finney, the great lawyer turned revivalist who died in 1875, understood that all aspects of society had to be changed in order for revival to take place. In his book *Freemasonry* he tells about the falseness of this secret order. It is said that he would even have Masons come to the altar and repent of their involvement in the group. This resulted in many of their lodges being closed down.

A former Mason himself, Finney writes of the oath they take in which they swear to what should happen to them if they ever tell an outsider the secrets of Masonry:

> *Binding myself under no less penalty than to have my throat cut across, my tongue torn out by its roots, and my body buried in the rough sands of the sea at low-water mark, where the tide ebbs and flows twice in twenty-four hours.*[7]

Finney saw this as no less than idolatrous and felt it was impossible to be both a Mason and a Christian at the same time.

This great revivalist was not afraid to speak out against evil in the society of his day in spite of possible recriminations. Finney wrote in his book that William Morgan, who was trying to expose Freemasonry, was drowned for revealing what was happening in secret.

Francis A. Schaeffer says in his book *A Christian Manifesto* that our culture, society, government, and law are in the condition they are in because the church has forsaken its duty to be the salt of the culture.[8]

As president of Oberlin College, Finney also took a strong stand against slavery. Oberlin was a stop on the Underground Railroad and a strong warrior in the fight against slavery in our society. In fact, while still a pastor in New York, Finney refused to allow slave owners to take Communion because he saw owning slaves as living in sin. Both he and the founder of Wheaton College in Massachusetts, Judge Laban Wheaton, believed in civil disobedience, when necessary, to change a nation.

CIVIL DISOBEDIENCE: THE CALL TO MORAL ACTIVISM

What did they mean by civil disobedience? It meant that when the laws of the nation oppose the laws of God, we ought to obey God and not man. *The Message* puts it like this in Acts 5:29: *"It's necessary to obey God rather than men."* I like that wording: "It's necessary." It implies that we have to, we must, we cannot live without or do anything less in our lives than obey God in every part of how we think and act in society.

What does this mean on a personal level? It means on moral issues, such as abortion, euthanasia, and sexual promiscuity in our society and in the entertainment industry, we need to speak out with a loud voice. We need to vote our convictions in national, state, and local elections, speak out for justice and righteousness, and be proactive in every way we can. The bottom line is this:

> **It is time for moral activism. We ought to obey God and not man. It is necessary as Christians to do so.**

There are times in the course of our lives when we see an evil and must not only speak out against it but take some moral action to publicly display our displeasure against it. This is the case for civil disobedience. When we can right a wrong, we need not look for another person to do something—we need to do something.

THE MARCH ON WASHINGTON

Civil disobedience has shaped the history of the United States. A young Quaker named Alice Paul led one of the first marches on Washington. She was arrested three times, jailed, and went on hunger strikes—all to fight for a constitutional amendment allowing women to vote.

The suffragists marched on Washington to make their point on Inauguration Day, March 3, 1913. The march was remarkably well organized with the colors of the rainbow assigned to women from differing walks of life. For instance, women artists wore shades of red. Wage earners marched together, as did farmers and homemakers. The march was also desegregated, which was unheard of in that day and time. A whole group of African American women from Howard University in Washington, D.C. marched together as a group, and others were dispersed among the crowd.

Finally, on June 4, 1919, Congress passed the amendment to grant women the right to vote. It was ratified in 1920, and that year women voted in a presidential election for the first time.

Rosa Parks refused to go to the back of a bus in Montgomery, Alabama and went to jail for it. That led to other marches on Washington, D.C. to fight against racism and segregation. The movement was called a "moral revolution for jobs and freedom." Probably the most famous speech from these marches took place on August 28, 1963, and was made by the fiery preacher Martin Luther King, Jr. In it he said:

> I say to you today, my friends, so even though we face the difficulties of today and tomorrow, I still have a dream. It is a dream deeply rooted in the American dream.
>
> I have a dream that one day this nation will rise up and live out the true meaning of its creed: "We hold these truths to be self-evident that all men are created equal."
>
> ...When we allow freedom to ring, when we let it ring from every village and every hamlet, from every state and every city, we will be able to speed up that day when all of God's children, black men and white men, Jews and Gentiles, Protestants and Catholics, will be able to join hands and sing in the words of the old Negro spiritual, "Free at last! free at last! thank God Almighty, we are free at last!"[9]

Do you have a God-given dream? You can make a change to see God's righteousness and justice released into His world. The call to become a reformer is about living your life each and every day in a way that God's will is done "on earth as it is in heaven." The great challenge to a humanist-based, liberal society is for Bible-believing citizens to screen their every thought and action through the Word of God and see God's miracles and presence again in our midst. Only when we manifest the true love of God in our own lives will those around us understand what they are missing without God's righteousness ruling their lives.

In the United States, Canada, and England, we at least have a memory of what a Christian society should look like, but the memory is fading fast. However, God's light is a bright light. It is stronger and more intense than any darkness Satan can gather. It is time to release that light into our culture again and chase out the darkness!

THE CLARION CALL

As I am writing the last pages of this book, I must confess that I have been experiencing a swirl of emotions. At times tears have flowed while I have thought of the enormity of the task at hand to see reformation in our nation. During my research for this book, I happened upon a little book edited by Bramwell Booth about the life of his mother, Catherine, who founded the Salvation Army with her husband, William.[10] A number of mornings I have crawled out of bed in the wee hours and wept through its pages. One passage struck me as I read sketches of her life and quotes from a eulogy written by her husband. These are the words from his lips about his beloved wife, who was struck down by cancer at age sixty-one:

> Lastly, she was a warrior. She liked the fight. She was not one who said to others, "Go," but "Here, let me go," and when there was the necessity, she cried "I will go!" I never knew her to flinch until her poor body compelled her to lay aside.[11]

Cowardice, in her opinion, was one of the commonest and subtlest sins of the day, and she had no patience with those who dared not say no and feared to stand alone. I have stood at the grave of this "Army Mother" with these and other words from her echoing in my heart. Cowardice? Never! One cannot change a nation from such a stance. She accepted the call of God that not only included the saving of souls but addressing the social ills of her nation. Can we do any less?

A few years ago some friends and I wrote a document in which we repented of the silence of Americans as the Holocaust decimated the Jews in Nazi Germany. We presented it along with a wreath at the Holocaust Museum in Washington, D.C. After the presentation, we toured the halls of remembrance together.

As we came to the end of the museum, I stood and read a statement written by Martin Niemoeller, who had been a Lutheran pastor like Dietrich Bonhoeffer in Germany prior to World War II:

> First they came for the Socialists, and I did not speak out—because I was not a Socialist. Then they came for the Trade Unionists, and I did not speak out—because I was not a Trade Unionist. Then they came for the Jews, and I did not speak out—because I was not a Jew. Then they came for me—and there was no one left to speak for me.

After I finished reading this, I stood transfixed, feeling strongly the Holy Spirit saying, "Don't think this cannot happen in your own nation."

There is a statement attributed to Edmund Burke: "All that is necessary for evil to triumph is for good men to do nothing." This is a time for all of us to do something to change our nations and see that God's will prevails. If not, there may be a day when we are forced to take a stand.

Rod Parsley heard a clarion call in the U.S. and founded the Center for Moral Clarity. In the introduction of his book *Silent No More*, he writes, "I will be silent no more. I must speak, and I must speak now. Our times demand it. Our history compels it. Our future requires it. And God is watching."[12]

God is watching, indeed. He understands costly grace and wants us His children to be just like Him. Is there not a just cause? We must answer yes in our generation, not only for ourselves but for our children and those who will come after them. They are counting on us, and we must not fail.

Chapter Eleven

REVIVAL AND REFORMATION

EVERY SEASON HAS a new emphasis the Lord will give to His people. As I have traveled around the world, whether I am in Asia or Africa or Australia, I am hearing the title of this chapter pouring out in sermons and in private conversations. The gist is that we now realize it is not enough to have a revival. We need to see a reformation come out of the revival. While there is not any new truth, biblically, there is restored truth. This restored truth of revival and reformation is especially important in order for us to fulfill the Great Commission and see the nations of the earth discipled and taught of the Lord.

What is revival?

> The word *revival* comes from the Latin word *revivere*, meaning to live, to return to consciousness, to reawaken or a renewal of fervour. ...So wrote G.J. Morgan in *Cataracts of Revival*.
>
> The Greek word for revival is *anazopureo*, which means to stir up or rekindle a fire which is slowly dying, to keep in full flame. It is used metaphorically when the apostle Paul wrote to Timothy, "...Stir up the gift of God which is in you..." (2 Timothy 1:6).[1]

Biblical reform means to return to a biblical worldview. Basically, it is the premise that God is the creator of the world, and so the principles, rules, and the revealed word of God need to be obeyed.

I especially love the theme of this chapter. Many prophetic voices are prophesying a great harvest of the earth is beginning. Some are even saying this could well be the end-time harvest before the Lord's return. I am aware that many generations have felt they were the last one and the Lord would come back in their lifetime. This isn't necessarily a bad thing. This longing for the Lord's imminent return presses us to reach the lost and reform our nations back to biblical truth.

The message of revival is very dear and close to my heart. My preacher daddy was fervent for revival. He was a church planter for the Southern Baptists, and everywhere he went he showed the love of God to the lost.

My daddy, the Rev. Albert S. Johnson, went to be with the Lord suddenly. He had a massive heart attack and was just gone at the age of 49. One day my sister and I were talking to him on the phone, and the next he was in heaven. Mike was my boyfriend then and he drove me from San Antonio, Texas to pick up his "effects" in San Marcos, Texas. His Bible was there, and the ribbon in his Bible was marked to Psalm 85:6:

> *Will You not revive us again, that Your people may rejoice in You?* (Psalm 85:6)

There was one sermon in his Bible. It was my daddy's notes on revival. Even to the last, he had revival on his heart.

We have spent a whole book talking about reformation. In this chapter, we will look at revivals and the impact they have made on society. Then, in the last chapter of this book, we will connect awakenings, reformation, and transformation. Transformation is the lasting fruit of a regional and worldwide awakening leading to reformation.

JESUS FREAKS

I lived through what has become known as The Jesus People Movement, as well as what is called the Charismatic Renewal. I am going to write more about the Charismatic Renewal in the last chapter because it was, in my opinion, an awakening, while The Jesus People Movement was more of a revival. I am aware the lines between what is called a revival and awakening are at times blurred, but I will focus on the revival aspect of The Jesus People Movement.

While studying at Grand Canyon College from 1969 to 1972, we had a revival and it impacted the whole school. At the same time, Arthur Blessitt had made a cross to hang on the wall of "His Place" on Sunset Strip in Hollywood. Arthur had been thrown out of his building on Sunset Strip, (or Sunset Blvd., as it is officially known). He then chained himself to a pole for 28 days to make a statement that he wasn't going anywhere.

We were known as "Jesus Freaks" and the "Jesus People," as we called ourselves. On a broad scale, it was known as *The Jesus Revolution*. Our sign was the index finger pointing to heaven. We wore Jesus People jewelry, gave the One-Way Jesus sign to each other in restaurants and public places. People, both saved and unsaved, recognized the sign. I will never forget going through a fast food line. The worker saw my Jesus jewelry and said out loud, "Are you one of those Jesus Freaks?" I proudly replied, "Why yes, I am!"

Basically, we were not ashamed to be called Christians. We were the visible church and loved it!

As a group of college students, we named our particular brand of Jesus People "The God Squad." On Saturday mornings, when we could, we would meet at the school in a room and worship. Someone brought a guitar, and then after that we would pray for God to give us direction on where to go to evangelize. We would pray for a particular neighborhood, and armed with tracts called *The Four Spiritual Laws* we would foray out from house to house and ring doorbells. Our endeavors were a roaring success as people in house after house read through our evangelistic tract with us and gave their hearts to the Lord.

Of course, we were only a small group, but our actions were multiplied many times over across the nation and the world. New music was written, such as "I Wish We'd All Been Ready" by Larry Norman. We avidly read Hal Lindsey's book *The Late Great Planet Earth*, about the soon return of the Lord. I know a man who got saved just reading the book. We expected Jesus to come at any moment. In fact, I remember one time in college when I felt down because I really thought I might not ever be able to get married before the Lord returned! Now going on 50 years of marriage, with two children and six grandchildren, I can see that was anguish I could have spared myself!

The movement started loosely in the later 1960s and '70s. Magazines from the time, such as *Look* and *Life*, proclaimed things like, "Look out, the Jesus People are coming!" *Time* and *Newsweek* also covered the movement.

During these years, a new newspaper called *The Hollywood Free Press* started. At its high point, it circulated some 500,000 copies. It was full of exciting Jesus People news.

Another distinctive of the movement was an emphasis on returning to the simple life. This movement rose up during what was known in North America as the hippie people and beatnik era. Some of the groups, such as the *Jesus Forever* group in Toronto, Canada, disdained a strong work ethic because they felt Jesus was returning soon and they needed to spend their time evangelizing. There was also a newspaper called *The Canadian Free Press*. Of course, a whole book could be written on this subject alone.

During this period, there was also something called the Summer of Love. It was an event held in 1967 in San Francisco, California. While God was unleashing His power to change the culture, there were other dark forces at work. It is estimated that 100,000 people participated in the Hippie Movement. They wore a particular style of clothing—flowers in the hair and loose, flowing garments. Their lifestyle included free sex, hippie bands, heavy use of drugs such as LSD, which were hallucinogenic, and anti-war slogans. They mainly settled in the Haight-Ashbury district of San Francisco. Other nations, such as Germany, followed their example and held their own *Summer of Love* events. The Jesus People Revolution ran counter-cultural to the hippie movement. People were set free, many very dramatically, from addictions and the darkness of sin in general.

I believe God sent the Jesus People Revival, among other reasons, to be a force to reform the impact of the Summer of Love to this nation and nations of the earth. The type of drugs that were being used were very destructive and primarily impacted youth and young adults. I know of a pastor who grew up in Haight-Ashbury and took drugs with his parents from the time he was a small child. When he was saved, he was set completely free of the addiction to drugs, and God restored his mind. He is a great Bible teacher today and influences a generation of young people.

A number of my friends today are guys who wore their hair really long in the hippie era, and not because they were Nazirites! (Nazirites in the Bible made a vow, or were called of God, not to cut their hair. Samson was a Nazirite.) It was simply the style, and even non-hippie people wore their hair longer than the close-cropped style of the last generation.

This brings up the point that revival movements are usually highly controversial. They are messy, and often stretch the bounds of what the church considers acceptable "church behavior." There have historically been physical manifestations and the breaking of religious norms, such as when Jesus healed on the Sabbath. It is easy to throw about the word *heretic* when something new is happening, but I encourage you not to be too quick to judge.

Sad to say, even though I grew up in a wonderful denomination, because it was non-charismatic I never even knew about some of the greatest revivals in the earth. For example, I didn't know about the Azusa Street Revival, which influenced the Jesus People Movement. Other great moves of God, such the healing revival under John G. Lake, were also completely unknown to me.

True revival also brings unity among believers. I remember this quote from Ed Silvoso about the Argentine Revival: "When the harvest grows so high, one cannot see the fences." An impactful prayer meeting I participated in during the revival in Resistencia in the Chaco province in Northern Argentina was one such fruit of unity. Pastors from many denominations were praying together. All of a sudden, a bass voice rang out. It was the pastor of the Baptist church. The translator quickly shared the interpretation of his significant prayer, "Lord, bless my brother's church more than mine!" He was clearly broken under the power of the Holy Spirit's leading.

When Ed Silvoso and Harvest Evangelism (now Transform Our World), started working in the city, sixty out of seventy of the churches in the city were formed through a church split. Ed's team, led by Dave and Sue Thompson, worked until the churches came together. Then, they all labored together to reach the whole city.

PLAN RESISTENCIA

This story can rightfully go in this chapter as well as the next one on awakening, reformation, and transformation. The Harvest team implemented a brilliant strategy called *Plan Resistencia*. It involved bringing mayors, judges, businesspeople, artists, etc. of the city to meet with other leaders like them. An explosion of creative ideas sprang forth from their meetings. Ed raised money to build a water well and a holding tank to meet the physical needs of the city.

At that time, evangelical Christians were considered a sect in the country. They could not serve as the president of the nation and were largely snubbed by politicians in general. Christians there said pastors would come to see the government leaders and wait and wait, until their appointments failed to materialize. (They found out later that the officials had "skipped" out the back door.) However, some thirty years later, the evangelicals have garnered such respect that when a candidate runs for office, they request to come visit the churches during a service.

One pastor who is a friend of mine, Rev. Jorge Ledesma, just recently built a building to seat 18,000 people and paid cash for the facility. The means he used to equip the facility were certainly reformational in thinking. For instance, that many chairs were very expensive, so they started their own chair-making factory on the grounds of the church site, made their own seats, and saved a lot of money!

Of course, one cannot discount the prayer side of this story. The Christians of Argentina are a praying people. I will delve into prayer for revival and awakening more in the next chapter.

When I first went to Resistencia, my job was to teach on spiritual warfare and pray over the strongholds of the city. At that time, the city was, spiritually speaking, a dark, dark area.

I will never forget the night Dave Thompson, I, Doris Wagner, Victor Lorenzo, and a few others went at midnight to pray in the plaza. Argentina at that time was in a terrible period of hyper-inflation. The streets were full of potholes, as were the sidewalks. However, Victor felt the powers of darkness were strongest at midnight. So of course, that is when we went!

We discovered panels placed in the park clearly showing both the visible and the invisible realms (see Rom. 1:20). One side of the panel showed a peaceful scene of farmers and fish in a river, and the other side was very dark with images of Kurupi, a very wicked sexual demon, and San la Muerte, the goddess of the dead. Kurupi had a large male organ and was responsible for all kinds of sexual mischief. San la Muerte was worshiped so people would have a good death.

After much prayer, we went back to pray at these panels to pull down the strongholds. It was a powerful time of prayer. What happened after these powers were dealt with? There were spikes in church growth, which meant a large number of people were saved. The darkness or veil that had been over the eyes of the lost was torn down, and the glorious light of the gospel was spread from person to person.

At the end of a large outdoor campaign, where evangelists such as Carlos Anacondia, the Rev. Omar Cabrera Sr., Ed Silvoso, and I preached, the power and glory of God fell! Many miracles broke out and hundreds were saved and received deliverance from demonic powers.

One night, at the suggestion of Doris Wagner (the widow of Peter Wagner and my traveling and ministry partner), the team got a large, metal oil drum. It was put there for people to throw in their witchcraft amulets, potions, fetishes, and the like to burn. This is a biblical practice:

Also, many of those who had practiced magic brought their books together and burned them in the sight of all. And they counted up the value of them, and it totaled fifty thousand pieces of silver (Acts 19:19).

As the witchcraft items burned, there were screams piercing the air as the people who had been connected to the objects manifested demons. There were teams spread throughout the crowd who would gather those who were oppressed and take them to the deliverance tent behind the platform.

One of the people who had come to help from a church in the U.S., where they weren't used to seeing such things, scoffed at people believing that the potions could hurt anyone. He found one of the bottles that had not burned and started putting the liquid on his neck mockingly. It was not very long until he had to be rushed to the hospital as his brain was swelling!

As I mentioned earlier, prayer and spiritual warfare were keys to the harvest. The intercessors would crawl under the high platforms and cry out to God. At times, when the anointing seemed to be waning as I preached, I would stomp on the wooden platform. That was the sign for the intercessors to rev up their praying. Unseen to the eyes of the crowd, there was a spiritual nuclear power plant underneath that platform. I could literally feel the vibration of their cries under my feet as they poured themselves out before the Lord.

One night as I preached, God gave me a prophetic word that there was a Macumba priest far out in the crowd in that big open field. There were thousands upon thousands there that night and I could not see anything in particular. However, I was later told that the word was true!

There was, indeed, a Macumba priest who had set up a portable altar, with lit candles, and was throwing some kind of substance into the wind, all the while muttering spells.

The word the Lord gave me that night was this, "There is someone here tonight trying to curse the meeting. It's not working!" The observer who reported to us said, "At that point, the priest blew out his candles and packed them away, along with his portable altar, and went home."

During the worship service, the favorite song for the healing service was "The Man from Galilee Is Passing Your Way!" The crowd would pull out white handkerchiefs and twirl them around.

What a sight that was, as thousands upon thousands of those handkerchiefs swirled through the night air!

And after that, the miracles! Miracles of every kind! My favorite one was when I was praying for the sick and I began to see a small child lifted up over people's heads and passed from hand to hand to the platform. She looked to be around five years old. The little one stood on her feet and gazed around in wonder and started walking up and down. People were hugging each other and crying. Everyone was speaking so fast in Spanish that I couldn't understand what they were saying.

Then, a woman came to the platform who appeared to be around sixty. She was crying—hard! At last, Mike and I received the testimony that the woman was the little one's *abuela,* or grandmother. Abuela had told her grandchild that when they went to the meeting that night, the Man from Galilee would heal her. It seems she had been paralyzed and wore a big body brace. When God gave me the word that someone in the crowd could not walk, and to stand up and walk in the Name of Jesus, she stood up and did just that! What a great rejoicing took place at the testimony.

There were many other miracles taking place also. A man with a metal plate in his head had it turn to bone. A little girl with crossed eyes saw them completely straighten. Another man had a knife wound completely healed.

Many people were saved during *Plan Resistencia*. The pastors brought water troughs, filled them using hoses, and held an outdoor baptism service.

This chapter is entitled "Revival to Reformation." What were some of the changes seen in the city and Chaco province?

- As I mentioned earlier, the influence of the church on public affairs changed 180 degrees from 1990, with inroads to city hall especially, and has continued to grow throughout the years.

- There are many Christians occupying local, city, and provincial posts.

- On the recent national abortion vote, six of the seven Chaco delegates voted pro-life (although the pro-abortion bill was passed in the congressional assembly).

- The Director of Public Health for the Province of Chaco is a born-again believer who began to dream of transformation for her city and province as a teenager when she heard Ed Silvoso and me and others during the *Plan Resistencia*.

- The current mayor of the city has enacted an open-door policy to the influence of evangelical leaders.

- *Transform Our World* has raised up young marketplace entrepreneurs, as well as government leaders, through their Christian Chamber of Commerce.[2]

THE WELSH REVIVAL

Many Christians have heard or read about the 1904 Welsh Revival under Evan Roberts. I had the privilege, along with my friend Kathryn VanSinderen, to go on a trip to Wales, along with the great revival historian, Michael Marcel. Michael has identified hundreds of wells of revival where revivals have taken place in the United Kingdom.[3] He has personally driven to the sites to do research and invested his own income into giving us the spiritual remembrances of revivals.

In studying the Welsh revival, there were significant meetings taking place prior to God setting Evan Roberts, a former coal miner, on fire for a move of God. There had been a call to prayer for revival starting in 1899 and continuing through 1903. God uses people in revival, and Evan was certainly the catalyst God used in such a large way in the Welsh Revival that he is the one most thought of regarding it.

The roots of Evan Roberts being touched by God came at a meeting in New Quay, Wales. Pastor Joseph Jenkins was preaching there in 1903 when a twenty-year-old, Florrie Evans, stood up to testify, saying, "I love the Lord Jesus Christ with all of my heart!" Somehow, those words were infused with the power of the Holy Spirit, and the conviction of sin fell in the place. It was reported that it was like an electric shock hit the room.

Two young women from this revival went to testify in Blaenannerch. It was there, in God's providence, Evan Roberts attended the meeting and cried out, "God, bend me!" (Meaning, literally, "fold me." He cried these words out loud while draped over the back of a wooden divider.) As I stood in that small church with my friends so many years later, I felt the power of the Holy Spirit in a massive way.

News of this meeting was reported in the *South Wales Daily News,* writing, "The third great revival was afoot through the nation!" The other two revivals were the Welsh Methodist Revival and the 1859 Methodist Revival.

Evan Roberts had a vision that God would save 100,000 through his preaching. He had prayed for thirteen years to see revival. The Lord often visited him at 1:00 a.m. and gave him visions, which he would share in his meetings. Hallmarks of the revival were open confession of sin, singing, and giving testimonies. Oh, but the Welsh can sing! Eventually, it is estimated that 100,000 people were saved in the first six weeks of the revival. According to Mathew Backholer in his book *Reformation to Revival,* this was just as Evan Roberts had seen in his vision. J. Edwin Orr stated he believes as many as 250,000 could have been converted during this revival.[4]

However, especially pertinent to this chapter, this revival through him and other preachers of the time led to a wonderful cultural revival. The newspapers in particular were used to spread the news of the move of God. *The Western Daily Mail* and the aforementioned *South Daily News* generated an air of excitement. *The Western Daily Mail* gave extensive coverage to Roberts' meetings in Loughor. The articles were gathered together and published in pamphlets. God wants to use journalists in a big way in the coming revivals around the world. Peter Wagner used to say that any move of God not written about is not remembered. We are indebted to those who have taken their time as publishers of the good news in various forms.

We have so many ways to get the gospel out today! I pray many who are reading this book will be called to write.

One important sociological effect, which was reformational in the culture, was many were convicted of drunkenness in the county of Glamorgan. That led to a nearly a 50 percent reduction of drunken behavior after the revival. This was critical to alleviate suffering in family structures as the children would have had food to eat and other necessities because money did not all go to alcohol consumption.

You may have heard stories about how the revival affected the coal miners. They stopped cursing and the pit ponies in the mines had to be re-trained because they did not recognize their new "clean" commands. Coal miners started their workdays on their knees in prayer. Sports games were affected also with the singing of hymns. Many new hymns were written for the revival, the most popular being "Here Is Love, Vast as the Ocean." That song is still sung in churches in Wales today. I was happy to have it sung for me when I preached in Wales.

A BBC religion article included paragraphs from newspapers at the time of the revival and its effects:

> Houses became decently furnished, women and children became decently clad. ...Bridges and walls, instead of being covered with obscene remarks, were now covered with lines from Bible and hymn book. The streets echoed with hymns, rather than the drunkard's songs once wont to be heard.[5]

Other things I noted that were reformational were the police were left with virtually nothing to do and the courts were empty. Old debts were paid in full. Revival broke out in a rugby match when 10,000 began singing hymns, and relationships and marriages were healed. Football players joined the street meeting to testify about Christ. Schools were touched by God's power. Basically, the revival touched most, if not all of the sectors of society, and the culture was reformed.

In the Rhondda valley and beyond, God convicted of sin, which eventually led to salvation, which brought about changed lives, sobriety, and restraint. On Christmas Eve in Abercarn, there was not a single summons to court. That had not happened since its formation some fourteen years previously. White gloves were handed out through the mayors of cities in memory of there being no cases the last day of 1904.[6]

I have personally been involved in revivals in various countries of the world. Most of them seem to last only a short while. In the coming revivals, we need to see them go on to cause a reformation in society. Teaching needs to take place on how to disciple the saved to "go into all the world and make disciples and teach nations." While salvation is eternal, learning how to be change agents in our societies and our need to be involved in Kingdom extending is essential after salvation to see the will of God to be done on the earth as it is in heaven.

I think we all need to cry out and ask God to bend us to His will 100 percent. My friend, Sergio Scatalingi, a great holiness preacher, says that we cannot think that if we are 98 percent holy, we will be where we need to be with God. Two percent poison will still kill us. We need to be 100 percent holy.

It is critical that we look into the subject of prayer awakenings and the coming of revivals and awakenings.

We are going to go deeper into these subjects in the final chapter of *Reformers Arise,* titled "Awakenings, Reformation, and Transformation."

Chapter Twelve

AWAKENINGS, REFORMATION, AND TRANSFORMATION

WE TALKED ABOUT revival and reformation in the last chapter. Now, we are going to move into awakenings that lead to reformation and, at last, to a state of transformation.

The lines between what is called a revival and an awakening are, as I mentioned in the last chapter, fairly blurry. Not all revivals are awakenings, but all spiritual awakenings are the result of revival. An awakening can be defined as a revival that becomes widespread to a region, nation, or even multiple nations. It is when the consuming fire of God burns across widespread areas. A true awakening will often lead to a reformation of societal morals.

Awakenings often begin with one or more people who see the moral depravity of their area or nation and include an intense burden for the salvation of souls. The often-quoted statement is true here: "The world has yet to see what God can do with one man or woman [inclusion of woman is mine] who is wholly consecrated to Him."

The Lord will often supernaturally draw a small group of dedicated friends or even family members together to pray and commit themselves to pursuing God, such as the Holy Club at Oxford.

The Holy Club consisted of just eight members in 1729 and was formed when its members were students at Oxford University. Brothers John and Charles Wesley and George Whitefield were among the most notable, although others in the group also went on to become revivalists. In studying this club, I was interested to note the derision that they suffered simply for wanting to seek God together in a regular way. The name *Holy Club* was actually a term of derision from their fellow classmates. The other mocking name they were called was *methodist*, because they had a "method" of reading together and discussing topics about God. They also celebrated communion at their meetings and fasted on Wednesdays and Fridays until 3:00 pm.

In addition to the Holy Club being a term of derision, so was the title of *methodists*. John Wesley wrote a letter about this name given to mock. He referred to the name given by them by saying, "Some of our neighbors are pleased to compliment us."[1] The name was used by an anonymous author in a pamphlet from 1733 describing Wesley and his group as "The Oxford Methodists."

I believe with all my heart that God is about to stir up many college students on campuses to raise up their own versions of the Holy Club. God will use covenant relationships that He draws together to fervency in praying, fasting, and reaching out to the lost once again. Perhaps you are one of those?

Some peg the start of the British Awakening to the date February 17, 1739, when George Whitefield chose an open field in which to preach to the coal miners in the area because there was no church in the region. (He had been a member of the Holy Club at Oxford with the Wesleys.) There were two hundred in attendance at the first meeting and the next it grew to 2,000!

One author wrote of this area: "Here lived a godless, ferocious race, men who lived beyond the pale of religion or even the law...they were a people apart, a byword for vice and crime.[2]

What happened in that field was truly a move of God. The meetings grew. As many as 20,000 came and they had to move to a larger field in Bristol. This went on for six weeks, and finally Whitefield prevailed to see if John Wesley would take over that work. John and Charles were also preaching in fields at that time. We do not think very much about them doing so, but these were not officially "sanctioned" meetings, and they were opposed for holding them.

It is said that George Whitefield preached 18,000 sermons in his lifetime; 30,000 came to his meetings at the Cambusiang Revival for a communion weekend. I was interested to find out the taking of communion was a part of some of these revivals. This is something that also occurred during the COVID-19 pandemic in the United States, when people started taking daily Holy Communion in their homes.

John Wesley preached 42,000 sermons, which was an average of fifteen per week for fifty-three consecutive years. Wesley was probably the most widely read person of his day, and he felt it his duty after reading a book to comment on it.

These men were consecrated for the work of the Lord, or one could say they were consumed by it. It was noted in some of the books I read that some became too passionate in the times of revival. They never rested and this adversely affected their health. This may have been the case with Evan Roberts who broke down after preaching so many times. He mostly left the preaching scene after his involvement in the Welsh revival. We must all remember we are human beings and not machines!

I would be completely remiss in this chapter if I did not write a section on probably my favorite aspect of any awakening—that of the role of prayer. Awakening prayer meetings, both pre-awakening and as a result of the awakenings of the prayer, are a foundation stone in their birthing and continued success.

In his book *The Great Prayer Awakening of 1857-58,* Eddie Hyatt writes of the prayer movement that "ended slavery and saved the American Union." It took place in history four years before the U.S. Civil War. Hyatt writes:

> For any revival to be called a Great Awakening, it should have the following three characteristics:
>
> 1. It is an obvious sovereign work of God in that it has arisen apart from any identifiable human plan, strategy or design.
>
> 2. It is non-sectarian and touches people of all sects and denominations. No one group, or church, can "own" the revival.
>
> 3. It is not localized or regional but has an obvious national impact on the nation and its culture."
>
> The Great Prayer Awakening of 1857-58 possessed these characteristics.[3]

J. Edwin Orr is famously quoted, "Whenever God is ready to do something new with His people, He always sets them praying."

One part of this prayer awakening was the moral outrage that grew out of the First Great Awakening. Whereas people had been insensitive, for the most part, to the plight of the slaves, the prayer awakening of this period awakened their hearts to injustice. Abraham Lincoln described the refusal of the founders to acknowledge slavery in the Constitution as being like a man who hides an ugly, cancerous growth until the time comes that it can be eradicated from his body.

Much has been written about the prayer awakening under Jeremiah Lanphier. This awakening has also been called the *Business People's Revival*. It started, as I mentioned before, in 1857.

Lanphier had been hired by the Dutch North Church on Fulton Street in Manhattan, New York to reach out to immigrant families. He was not an evangelist, but rather a businessman. He at first tried to hand out gospel tracts and evangelize. Most people were, at best, indifferent to his efforts. At first he was discouraged, but then felt led of the Lord to start a prayer meeting. Of course, history shows that prayer meeting became a prayer awakening.

Let me stop and share a point with you. Great awakenings are sometimes preceded by the potential for great disappointments and discouraging situations. When you are pressing toward God, the roadblocks in your way are only temporary. At times, you might even have fallen flat on your face in your endeavors. When this happens, as John Maxwell has said, *"Fail forward."*

Jeremiah then had an inspiration, which proved to be from God. He began passing out handbills inviting businessmen to come and pray for the lost during their lunch breaks.

At the first prayer meeting on September 23, 1857, there did not seem to be anything that would forecast the great move of God it precipitated. Six people showed up. Not an auspicious beginning, to say the least!

The next prayer meeting had swelled to twenty-five and the group decided to make it a daily event. In a week, more than a hundred attended. God's timing was perfect, as always, as the week after that the worst economic crisis in American history took place.

This crisis was the spark that caused intense spiritual hunger. Many pastors started opening their churches for prayer, and then the spark became a full-fledged flame. It spread to other cities and the newspapers considered it front-page news.

The meetings were held during the noon hour and had a simple format of taking requests for prayer with no prayer to be more than five minutes long. The power of conviction began to spread to those they prayed for and they began to come under the convicting power of God. Charles Finney, the great evangelist himself, would tell stories about what had happened during the meetings. D.L. Moody as a young man attended prayer meetings like this in Chicago and noted the presence of God. It is fascinating to me how the next generation is deeply impacted to go all out for God by attending prayer gatherings hosted by the generation before them.

For example, in a noon prayer meeting at a church in downtown Kalamazoo, Michigan, the crowd was standing room only. A prayer request was read from a wife asking for prayer for her unsaved husband. Immediately, a man stood to his feet and with tears exclaimed, "I am that man. My wife is a good Christian woman and she must have sent that request. Please pray for me!" He sat down and immediately a man in another part of the house stood to his feet weeping and, as if he had not heard the first man, declared, "That was my wife who sent that request. She is a good Christian woman and I have treated her badly. Please pray for me!" He sat down and another man stood, also convinced that it was his wife who sent the prayer request, and after him a fourth and fifth with similar confessions.[4]

While I could find little of the personal life of Jeremiah Lanphier prior to his being hired by the North Dutch Reformed Church, simply reading about the persistence, tenacity, and ability to gain a strategy from God on how to structure the prayer meetings during that time tells me volumes about him as a person. I have found one does not simply start something that becomes a prayer awakening that sparks around a million souls coming to Christ without an intimate knowledge of God.

Sean Smith, in his excellent book on revival *I Am Your Sign*, quotes G.J. Morgan's *Cataracts of Revival* about the preparation of the revivalist:

> God is always preparing His workers in advance; and when the hour is ripe, He brings them upon stage; and men look and wonder upon a career of startling triumph which God had been preparing for a lifetime. God is preparing His revivalists still, so when the opportunity comes He can fit them into their places in a moment, while the world wonders where they came from.[5]

Revivalists are awakeners. They not only win the lost but they awaken the church to its backslidden state and lack of passion and fire. Open confession of sin by believers often breaks open the heavens, and God then begins to pour out His Spirit upon cities and nations.

Smith also quotes Keith Hardman about awakenings:

> Awakenings begin in periods of cultural distortion and great personal stress, when we lose faith in the legitimacy of our norms, the viability of our institutions, and the authority of our leaders in church and state.[6]

In other words, when all around us our nations are falling into disrepair, the young people are disillusioned, people have left God out of the culture, and all seems dark, God comes on the scene. He sends revivalists and awakeners and has already been working behind the scenes to train up reformers who will see that God is preeminent in every aspect (or mountain or society).

Becoming an awakener requires giving 100 percent to God without holding anything back. A revival and awakening without a reformation usually lasts a short span of time—anywhere from a year to a decade. When people are trained with the biblical understanding that we must also become disciples of our nations, then it lasts and becomes transformation.

It is key here to learn from the testimony of a missionary named Edith Moules. Edith was from Britain and started as a maid in the home of a pastor. Then she went to Bible school for two terms and left a failure, according to the account of the *Dictionary of African Christian Biography*. She at last took a course on nursing, studied French, and went on a boat to the Belgian Congo in 1927.

She went on to pioneer medical missions among the leper colonies, which was really not something she wanted to do at all because of her fear of contracting the disease. God finally made it clear to her that she should conquer her fear and begin treating "the least of these" who were leprous.

Within a few months of starting their treatments, she had cared for 5,000 of those who were infected. After this, many came to Christ, and there was the need to plant churches in the leper colonies. The results were transformational among the people who had been largely abandoned and left without hope.

I use her life's story to bring home the point that no one is untouchable for those called to proceed from awakening to reformation to transformation. There are many stories of missionaries whose work among various people groups led from their becoming believers, to reformation, and then on to transformation. The Puritans who first came to Massachusetts Bay had a picture of an

Indian on their seal with the biblical phrase, *"Come and help us"* (Acts 16:9).

One such was the Rev. John Eliot, known as the "Apostle to the Indians." Eliot understood that while he could teach the natives the Word of God, they needed to be able to read it in their own language. The problem was, the Algonquin tribe didn't have a written language.

He then undertook to fix this problem himself and developed a written language. It took him twelve years of his life to do so and translate the Bible into the Algonquin. When it was printed, it became the first Bible to be printed on America soil.

Thank God for Wycliff Bible translators and others who carry on this work, as there are, as of this writing, some 3,000 languages with no written records of any type.

I remember William Booth of the Salvation Army once made a statement: *"Sometimes the need is the call."* Rather than needing five poems written on your bedroom wall and four visions to tell you how to start being a change agent, there are things that need to be done for the cause of Christ. Start by cleaning up the trash in a neighborhood or volunteering at a food bank. Find the need and fill it.

There have been times in American history when it was understood that the Bible was the tool God provided as the basis for societal norms and the common good for the underpinnings of the nation. In other words, our founders knew in order for the nation to be sustained as a republic throughout the centuries, its leaders needed to abide by biblical principles. It was noted that in order to be a public servant, one must know the Bible. This would be the salt that would keep the savor of the nation and keep it a moral and ethical nation. Its elected officials needed to not only be able and willing to read God's Word, but to read God's world (or nation) in the light of God's Word.

This was so front and center in the history of the U.S. that the congress had a special congressional committee convened to decide whether or not it was quicker to print or import Bibles so that the public schools would not be in danger of a Bible shortage in the classrooms. It was recommended:

> The use of the Bible is so universal and its importance so great...your Committee recommends that Congress will order the Committee of Commerce to import 20,000 Bibles from Holland, Scotland, or elsewhere, into the different ports of the States of the Union.[7]

This could not be enacted, because Congress had to be disbanded soon after the fact as the British landed in Philadelphia. It was reformation that reached the highest places of government.[8]

I am personally encouraged by the numbers of people who are teaching on how to disciple and teach nations in the church today. We are seeing signs here and there of Christians understanding their role to win souls and be reformers.

TRANSFORMATION

The title of this chapter is "Awakenings, Reformation, and Transformation." The reason I include transformation in a book on reformation is I believe that it is possible to teach one generation to "watch over" the next in such a way that a nation can be transformed. I am not talking about a utopian philosophy, but rather that Jesus really meant it when He gave us the commission to make disciples of nations.

A nation discipled and taught of the Lord would be a transformed nation. While we have seen a few nations reach what could be called a state of transformation for a season, it does not seem to stay transformed. However, this should not stop us from working toward that goal. The United States has certainly been a nation discipled and taught by the Lord at various points of our history.

My friend, George Otis Jr., produced the award-winning *Transformation* documentaries that, as of 2018, have been viewed by at least 250 million people in 17 nations. Otis, as we noted earlier, says in his history of studying 450 years of revival, transforming revival is the inevitable consequence of fervent, united, and prevailing prayer.[9] (By the way, if you have not watched this video series, I highly recommend that you do. Mike and I worked behind the scenes in a few of the nations highlighted, and we can also vouch for the fervency of the people's prayers.)

George Otis, along with Ed Silvoso, are two of the most notable people who have worked in the area of the transformation of nations. George Otis convened a group of leaders for a roundtable discussion on transformation in the early 2000s. The main topic was to discern how to see a lasting transformation of a nation.

Of course, these steps are tied to revival and awakening. Otis uses the phrase *transformational revival*. When revival comes, hearts are convicted of sin. God visits and gives correction to His people. This is at times both glorious and terrible.

Once we see a revival and awakening, then it is up to the leaders in the movement to see that there are further steps set in place to reform the nation. This needs to be done in a more intentional manner than we have done in the past.

Awakenings change people's hearts on a large scale, and often the churches grow quite large. If leaders aren't trained in advance for these visitations, then all the church can do is try and put in the necessary programs on how to teach new believers how to live the Christian life on a daily basis. However, it must go beyond that. We must teach them how to leave the church mountain and go out into every other mountain, become a reformer, and bring societal transformation.

If we do not do this, other religions will begin to come in and take our harvest fields. Intercession ripens the harvest, but the fields fall into decay if we do not become laborers in the fields.

According to George Otis, nearly all Christians readily agree with what God can do on a personal level. Nearly all Christians readily acknowledge that God transforms broken lives through the renewing of the mind. They also accept He works with families (recasting relational dysfunction into models of mutual respect and support) and with churches (replacing forms of godliness with genuine spiritual life and power). However, believers are far less certain when the conversation turns to the transformation of neighborhoods, cities, and regions.[10]

Otis goes on to list community transformation indicators:

1. Political leaders publicly acknowledge their sin and dependence on God.

2. New laws, curricula, and business practices are put into effect.

3. The natural environment is restored to its original, life-nurturing state.

4. Economic conditions improve and lead to a discernible lessening of poverty.

5. There is a marked change in social entertainment and vices as kingdom values are integrated into the rhythm of daily life.

6. Volunteerism increases as Christians recognize their responsibility to heal and undergird their community.

7. Restored hope and joy leads to a decline in divorce, bankruptcy, and suicide.

8. The spiritual nature of the growing socio-political renewal becomes a hot topic in the secular media.

9. Overwhelmed by the goodness of God, grateful Christians take the embers of revival into surrounding communities and nations.

10. Societal change (transformation/reformation) is a specific result or destination. The Holy Spirit will be doing His reviving work long before transformation becomes visible.[11]

Ed Silvoso, my dear friend, as I mentioned earlier, is one of the major pioneers in the area of transformation as well. Peter Wagner called him a "world-class missiologist." Ed is not a theoretician but rather a transformation practitioner. He has the ability to work with believers from all walks of life and raise them up to be powerful transformers in their cities and nations. One of the biggest challenges to the ordinary believer today is the belief that they cannot make a difference in their nation. In fact, awakenings, reformations, and transformations begin with ordinary people believing that they can do extraordinary things for God.

I personally do not believe that there are any ordinary Christians—only ones who need to understand that they can make a difference. You can make a difference!

Ed's ministry, Transform Our World, has many success stories of everyday people deciding to make a difference. One that I particularly love involved the transformation of a brothel in the Philippines. This hotel was particularly "successful." The motel chain consisted of eight buildings with 1,600 rooms. It employed 2,000 workers. Each room was used an average of five times a day by 3,000 prostitutes who, in cahoots with the management, "processed" around 15,000 "clients."[12]

The owner of the hotel knew he had to change things. He hired 30 pastors to pray for and minister to the needs of his employees. He built a prayer chapel in every hotel and informed the people as they checked in that prayer was available for them. Couples had to show a marriage certificate in order to check in. The result of their many efforts was that within eighteen months, more than 10,000 clients had come to know the Lord.

In order to be a reformer/transformer, the leaders of tomorrow need to be taught by the leaders of today how to not only see to one's personal needs but the needs of society. In other words, there are systemic issues we need to put our brightest minds to work on. They need to find biblical solutions that will work to eliminate such issues as systemic poverty. They need to develop models of biblical economic systems that provide solutions. The church needs the answers to not only biblical justice issues (i.e., fighting human trafficking and stopping abortion), but it needs to find solutions to matters such as food insecurity. It is hard to minister to someone who is hungry! One must first feed them![13]

> *Now all who believed were together, and had all things in common, and sold their possessions and goods, and divided them among all, as anyone had need* (Acts 2:44-45).

> *Nor was there anyone among them who lacked; for all who were possessors of lands or houses sold them, and brought the proceeds of the things that were sold* (Acts 4:34).

Silvoso writes in his book *Transformation* that in Acts 2:44-46 we see an uncommon reconciliation between the rich and the poor.

He goes on to say that people gave extravagantly to the poor, which reflected a dramatic change of attitude on their part—away from using their wealth to dominate and toward using the same to show godly deference. The fact that they fellowshipped daily and in homes shows that it was part of their lifestyle and not a function they participated in sporadically.[14]

This is by no means advocating far-left socialism. Communism and socialism are counterfeit institutions in regard to eradicating systemic poverty.

Believe it or not, there are areas in large cities, even my own Dallas, Texas, where there exists something called "food deserts." We are to be solution-providers for these desperate needs.

There are exciting works being started, such as those who have started organic gardens, like Bonton Farms, right in the middle of poverty. Bonton is the area of Dallas where the Freedmen were settled after slavery ended. However, it was a flood zone, there was no running water, and no public transportation to get to work. Enter Daron Babcock. He left a well-paying job in the financial sector to move into the neighborhood. He was a white guy who passionately loved the poor. He came with his wife and moved into a derelict house. His wife died of cancer, but he stayed on. It was simply horrible for him at times.

He led the local residents to plant organic vegetables. They grew fruit and made preserves. They have added the tending of bees, goats, and chickens. While it is non-profit, it is also self-sustaining as they have a market that sells their vegetables. They also supply their own farm-to-market restaurant. They hire former felons and give people a chance to start over. As of now, they are planting around 50 acres in produce. Urban gardens feed people and that feeds their souls as well.

Another organization, Habitat for Humanity, has built around 400 or so houses in the area as well. The city of Dallas also built some lovely housing. Sometimes it only takes someone to begin to do something that starts the transformation process. Bonton Farm's visionary, Daron, says, "It all starts with a seed." Another African organization called Farming God's Way is doing an incredible job around the world to help eliminate food poverty. This not only feeds people's bodies but provides a renaissance of hope for their souls.

This brings me to share my last point in this book. (Each of these many points are worthy of a book written just about them, and there are some excellent ones!) We are to live a transformational supernatural life. The testimony of a notable miracle has the power to cause individuals, families, and oftentimes whole villages to become transformed. There have been physical healings of someone well known in the community. At other times, angelic protections have been made visible to those who are attempting to take the life of a believer.

The history of world missions is full of God intervening in supernatural ways that opened various cultures' hearts to the gospel. They happen on a broad scale, from medical missions to great authority over the powers of darkness to physical healings to God, as mentioned before, sending angels to protect missionaries.

One of the most impacting missions books I have read is called *Before We Kill and Eat You,* subtitled *Tales of Faith in the Face of Certain Death*, as told to Ruthanne Garlock by the missionary H.B. Garlock.

In the foreword to the book, the great revival broadcaster C.M. Ward says of H.B. Garlock that he was one of the last missionaries who entered the mission field and survived by the power of the Holy Spirit alone. What he experienced in Africa could well be an additional chapter to the book of Acts.

He went on to write that H.B. and his wife, Ruth, "faced the raw power of wickedness, intertribal warfare, cannibalism, the incantations of hell, and the gloom and despair of centuries of superstition."[15]

The Garlocks went to Liberia when that nation was considered the graveyard of missionaries. A good percentage of the missionaries died from malaria within a relatively short time of going on the field. There are so many supernatural stories in this book, I just say you need to read it for yourself! However, I will give a few examples so you will understand my point of transformation.

One chief, after hearing of the claims that Jesus was a healer, said to Garlock:

> White man, you have asked us to give up the religion of our ancestors for a new religion, one that has not been tried by our people. ...We are prepared to consider serving your God, but before doing so we would like to see a demonstration of this power you talk about. There are many lepers in our village, would you mind healing some of them? ...There are many blind among us. Please heal some of these. And our people are dying every day.[16]

A woman had given birth and not been able to recover, and also had contracted leprosy in the village of Gredeji and died. Instead of burying their dead, they would put the body in a fetish grove and lay it on a refuse heap of skeletons and bodies. She had no heartbeat, but the missionaries had been believing for miracles and decided to take the step of faith and pray for her to be raised from the dead. The missionaries knelt on the dung heap and prayed out loud for all to hear. Ruth Garlock laid hands on the body and rebuked the spirit of death. To the shock of all who watched, the woman's body began to shake violently and was lifted up like she was levitating. The gathered crowd scattered. Suddenly, the shaking ceased, and the formerly dead woman sat up and asked for food.

Three weeks later, H.B. visited the hut of the husband of the woman to find out how she was doing, and he said that she was not there. He inquired as to where she was and was told she was in the fields working. To H.B.'s astonishment, the woman came up shortly with a huge load of firewood on her head, and on top of that was a stalk of bananas!

As a result, the chief, named Jufuli, who had challenged the missionaries to "heal a few people" renounced fetish worship as did most of the members of his council.

What were the results of them accepting Christ? Of course, the most important one is the eternal one. However, the missionaries were able to persuade the people not to sacrifice their children to idols, to institute good sanitation methods, allow their children to be educated, bring in modern medicine, and deliver the people from being controlled through fetish worship. They also gave up cannibalism and other atrocious practices.

God wants to do these three things throughout the earth: awaken, reform, and transform. These things are connected together. I believe we are already in the beginning stages of all three. The Lord is just looking for people He can count on to give their lives on an everyday basis to see these manifest throughout the earth—to see *His Kingdom come and His will be done.*

It is doable, and it is possible. God is just looking for willing hearts and hands to make it happen. You can be an awakener who is led to becoming, on a daily basis, a reformer who brings transformation. Now, be bold, and go do it!

NOTES

NEW INTRODUCTION

1. This was rectified in 2015 by the Spanish Parliament when they passed a law recognizing the descendants of the Jews expelled in 1492 as Spanish citizens. It was, however halted in 2019.
2. Lindy Lowry, "The 10 most dangerous places for Christians," Open Doors, January 15, 2020, https://www.opendoorsusa.org/christian -persecution/stories/the-10-most-dangerous-places-for-christians.

CHAPTER ONE

1. "Questions and Answers About Germany: Health Care, Health Issues and Social Welfare: Is Abortion Legal?" German Embassy Website, www.germany.info/relaunch/info/facts/questions_en/ health/healthissues3.html (accessed February 23, 2007).
2. "Historical Abortion Statistics, FR Germany," Johnston's Archive, updated February 18, 2007, www.johnstonarchive.net/policy/ abortion/ab-frgermany.html (accessed February 23, 2007).
3. "German Abortion Percentages by State, 1999-2004," Johnston's Archive, updated July 20, 2005, www.johnstonarchive.net/policy/ abortion/germany/ab-ges2.html (accessed February 23, 2007).

4. "Martin Luther: Passionate Reformer," Christian History and Biography website, www.christianitytoday.com/history/special/131christians/luther.html (accessed February 26, 2007).

5. For a more complete understanding of the intercessory role in healing nations, please read my book *Possessing the Gates of the Enemy* (Grand Rapids, MI: Chosen Books, 1994), especially chapter 2.

6. Max Weber, with Peter Baehr and Gordon C. Wells, translators, *The Protestant Ethic and the Spirit of Capitalism and Other Writings* (New York: Penguin Books, 2002).

7. "The White Rose," The Shoah Education Project website, www.shoaheducation.com/whiterose.html (accessed March 5, 2007).

8. Annette E. Dumbach and Jud Newborn, *Shattering the German Night: The Story of the White Rose* (New York: Little, Brown, and Company, 1986), quoted in Vicky Knickerbocker, *Study Guide for Sophie Scholl: The Final Days* (Minneapolis: Outreach Coordinator at the Center for Holocaust and Genocide Studies, University of Minnesota, 2006), 4.

9. "The White Rose," The Shoah Education Project website.

10. "Battle of Stalingrad," Wikipedia, the free encyclopedia, updated February 28, 2007, http://en.wikipedia.org/wiki/Battle_of_Stalingrad (accessed February 28, 2007).

11. Society of the White Rose, "Leaflets of the Resistance," The Sixth Leaflet, www.jlrweb.com/whiterose/leafsixeng.html (accessed March 1, 2007).

12. Jacob G. Hornberger, "The White Rose: A Lesson in Dissent," Jewish Virtual Library, www.jewishvirtuallibrary.org/jsource/Holocaust/rose.html (accessed February 28, 2007).

13. Ibid.

14. Richard Hanser, *A Noble Treason: The Revolt of the Munich Students Against Hitler* (New York: G.P. Putnam's Sons, 1979), 279-80.

15. Hornberger, "The White Rose."

16. Traudl Junge, *Blind Spot: Hitler's Secretary*, DVD, directed by Andre Heller and Othmar Schmiderer (Culver City, CA: Sony Pictures, 2002).

CHAPTER TWO

1. A.K. Curtis, "A Golden Summer," www.zinzendorf.com/agolden .htm (accessed April 19, 2007). This article first appeared in Glimpses from the Christian History Institute.

2. Jim W. Goll, *The Lost Art of Intercession* (Shippensburg, PA: Destiny Image, 1997), 3-4.

3. "John Huss," www.greatsite.com/timeline-english-bible-history/ johnhus.html (accessed April 20, 2007).

4. David L. Brown, "John Huss," http://logosreorcepages.org/ History/huss_b.htm (accessed April 20, 2007).

5. "John Huss," www.greatsite.com/timeline-english-bible-history/ johnhus.html (accessed April 20, 2007)

6. John Foxe, Foxe's Book of Martyrs, www.everydaycounslor.com/ archives/sh/hus2.htm (accessed April 20, 2007).

7. "Martin Luther," Wikipedia, the free encyclopedia, updated April 20, 2007, http://en.widipedia.org/wiki?Martin_Luther (accessed April 20, 2007).

8. C. Peter Wagner, *Confronting the Powers* (Ventura, CA: Regal Books, 1996), 32.

9. Ibid., 32-33.

10. Gilbert Bilezikian, *Beyond Sex Roles* (Grand Rapids: Baker, 1985, 214, quoted in David Cannistraci, *The Gift of Apostle* (Ventura, CA: Regal Books, 1996), 86.

CHAPTER THREE

1. *Nelson's New King James Version Study Bible* (Nashville: Thomas Nelson, 1997), 5.

2. I wish to express my gratitude to Landa Cope, the first one whom I heard speak about this concept from Scripture of God giving His people a plan for the sectors of society. I honor and thank her for the initial ideas she taught in South Africa at the Congress on World Evangelism that set me on this path of discovery.
3. We know this Book of the Law today as the first five books of the Old Testament. The Jewish people call it the Torah.
4. *New Spirit-Filled Life Bible* (Nashville: Thomas Nelson, 2002), commentary on 2 Kings 22:8-10, 511.

Chapter Four

1. Darrow L. Miller, with Stan Guthrie, *Discipling Nations: The Power of Truth to Transform Cultures*, 2nd edition (Seattle, WA: Youth with a Mission Publishing, 2001), 25.
2. Alvin Toffler, *Future Shock* (New York: Random House, 1970), 139.
3. "Joseph Fletcher," Wikipedia: the free encyclopedia, last modified June 5, 2007, http://en.wikipedia.org/wiki/Jospeh_Fletcher (accessed August 29, 2007).
4. J.I. Packer, "Situation Ethics," The Highway, www.the-highway.com/articleJan02.hml (accessed August 28, 2007). The quotation within is from Joseph Fletcher's *Situation Ethics: The New Morality* (Philadelphia: Westminster Press, 1966), 65. The italics are Fletcher's.
5. Joseph F. Fletcher, *Moral Responsibility: Situation Ethics at Work* (Philadelphia: Westminster Press, 1967), 138.

Chapter Five

1. C. Peter Wagner, *The Church in the Workplace* (Ventura, CA: Regal Books, 2006), 14.
2. R.E. Schofield, "The Lunar Society of Birmingham," *Scientific American* 247 (June 1982), quoted in Caryl Matrisciana and Roger

Oakland, *The Evolution Conspiracy* (Eugene, OR: Harvest House, 1991), 58.

3. Ian T. Taylor, *In the Minds of Men: Darwin and the New World Order* (Toronto: TFE Publishing, 1984), 55-57, 67, 120, quoted in Matrisciana and Oakland, *The Evolution Conspiracy*, 58-59.

4. "Naturalism," Wikipedia: the free encyclopedia, updated September 19, 2007, http://en.wikipedia.org/wikiNaturalism (accessed September 20, 2007).

5. Dennis Gordon Lindsay, *The ABCs of Evolutionism* (Dallas, TX: Christ for the Nations Publishing, 1995), 228-289.

6. Matt Crenson "On Ancestral Trails: Conflicting Evidence Muddies Path for Scientists Tracking Human Origins," *The Dallas Morning News*, May 9, 1994, http://nl.newsbank.com.

7. One of the best books I have found on this subject is Dave Breese's *Seven Men Who Rule the World from the Grave* (Chicago: Moody Publishers, 1990).

8. Humanist Manifesto, American Humanist Society, 1933, www.americanhumanist.org/about/manifesto1.html (accessed September 13, 2007).

9. Humanist Manifesto II, American Humanist Society, 1973, www.americanhumanist.org/about/manifesto2.html (accessed September 13, 2007).

10. Ibid.

11. Joseph Ratner, *John Dewey's Philosophy* (New York: Modern Library, 1939), 715, quoted in Breese, *Seven Men Who Rule the World from the Grave*, 165.

12. John Dewey, "My Pedagogic Creed," *The School Journal*, Vol. LIV, No. 3:16 (January 1997): 77-80, quoted in Jim Nelson Black, *Freefall of the American University* (Nashville, TN: WND Books, a division of Thomas Nelson Publishers, 2004), 85.

13. Charlotte Thomas Iserbyt, *The Deliberate Dumbing Down of America: A Chronological Paper Trail* (Ravenna, OH: Conscience Press, 1999), quoted in Black, *Freefall*, 86.

14. Chester M. Pierce, Keynote address, The Association for Childhood Education International, Denver, 1972, quoted in Black, *Freefall*, 87.
15. "The New England Primer," Wikipedia, the free encyclopedia, updated September 8, 2007, http://en.wikipedia.org/wiki/The_New_England_Primer (accessed September 13, 2007).
16. "McGuffey Readers," Wikipedia, the free encyclopedia, updated August 26, 2007, http://en.wikipedia.org/wiki/McGuffey_Readers (accessed September 13, 2007).
17. Black, *Freefall*, 192, 193.

CHAPTER SIX

1. Francis A. Schaeffer, *A Christian Manifesto* (Wheaton, IL: Crossway Books, 1981), 99.
2. Ibid., 100.
3. James Strong, *Enhanced Strong's Lexicon* (Ontario: Woodside Bible Fellowship, 1996), #4941, *mishpat*.
4. Ibid., #6666, *tsadaqah*.
5. "William Blackstone," From Revolution to Reconstruction, updated May 5, 2003, www.let.rug.nl/usa/B/blackstone.htm (accessed August 28, 2007).
6. David Barton, *Original Intent* (Aledo, TX: Wallbuilders Publishing, 1996, 2000), 53.
7. Ibid., 14.
8. Ibid., 119.
9. There are some magnificent studies of biblical law. Some of them are quite controversial, but should not be dismissed without an in-depth look at them—particularly by those in law. One of these is *The Institutes of Biblical Law* by Rousas John Rushdoony.

CHAPTER SEVEN

1. Accounts of this address can be found online at www.brycchancarey
    .com/abolition/wilberforce2.htm (accessed September 5, 2007).
2. Clifford Hill, *The Wilberforce Connection* (Oxford, UK: Monarch
    Books, 2004), 53.
3. Michael Hennell, *John Venn and the Clapham Sect* (London:
    Lutterworth Press, 1958), 169, quoted in Hill, *The Wilberforce
    Connection*, 47.
4. Quoted in Hennell, *John Venn*, 179; quoted in Hill, *The Wilberforce
    Connection*, 51.   As you can see, I am indebted to Clifford Hill's
    wonderful *The Wilberforce Connection* for his valuable research on
    this subject. My friend Lady Susie Sainsbury gave it to me while
    I was visiting her home, as I was planning to write a book on the
    subject of reformation. Thank you, Clifford and Susie!
5. Hill, *The Wilberforce Connection*, 28.
6. Stephen McDowell and Mark Beliles, *Liberating the Nations*
    (Charlottesville, VA: Providence Foundation, 1995), 64.
7. Miller, *Discipling Nations*, 139 (see ch. 4, n. 1)
8. Charles Colson and Nancy Pearcey, *How Now Shall We Live?*
    (Wheaton, IL: Tyndale House Publishers, Inc., 1999), 171.
    Colson and Pearcey do an excellent job of defining the effect that
    Rousseau had on revolution and society.
9. While I am speaking quite strongly against the principles of the
    French Revolution with regard to Rousseau's teaching, I am also
    strongly for the French people and feel that in looking at this
    subject we must also keep in our minds and hearts the great work
    the Huguenots did for religious freedom.
10. Michael Crichton, "Why Politicized Science Is Dangerous,"
    Appendix A: State of Fear (New York, Harper Collins, 2004),
    575-80.
11. McDowell and Beliles, *Liberating the Nations*, 54.

12. James S. Bell Jr. and Tracy Macon Sumner, *The Reformation and Protestantism* (Indianapolis, IN: Alpha Books, 2002), 157.
13. Luis E. Lugo, ed., *Religion, Pluralish, and Public Life* (Grand Rapids, MI/Cambridge, UK: William B. Eerdmans Publishing Co., 2000), 56.
14. Abraham Kuyper, "Calvinism and Romanticism," in Lugo, *Religion*, 53.
15. Aleksandr Solzhenitsyn, "Men Forgotten God," *National Review* (July 22, 1983), 872, quoted in Breese, *Seven Men*, 74 (see ch. 5, n. 7).
16. Charles Colson has started an amazing forum for training such leaders in his Centurions program. He states the need for such training while quoting George Barna—only 9 percent of believers have a biblical worldview of moral absolutes. For more information, see their website at: www.breakpoint.org/generic.asp?ID=2748 (accessed September 7, 2007).

Chapter Eight

1. James Strong, *England Strong's Lexicon* (Ontario: Woodside Bible Fellowship, 1996) #H7235, s.v., "rahbah."
2. Ibid., #4390, s.v., "mala."
3. Ibid., #3533, s.v., "kabash."
4. *Nelson's New King James Version Study Bible* (Nashville, TN: Thomas Nelson, 1997), 6.
5. Strong, #7287, s.v., "radah."
6. *Nelson's NKJV Study Bible.*
7. Miller, *Discipling Nations*, 114.
8. Tom Rose, *Economics: Principles and Policy from a Christian Perspective* (Mercer, PA: American Enterprise Publications, 1986), 33-34.
9. My thanks to Jerry Tuma of Cornerstone Financial Services for the information in this section.

10. By the way, Keynes was an atheist and a Fabian socialist who believed all the world's problems would one day be solved by a global, socialist government. We must view the world through the lens of an unlimited God, not temporary limitations to our supply of resources.

11. *The American Heritage Dictionary of the English Language*, 4th edition (Boston: Houghton Mifflin Company, 2006), s.v., "usury."

12. Dr. Gary North has some interesting comments on money and banking in his book *Honest Money: Biblical Principles of Money and Banking* (Arlington Heights, IL: Christian Liberty Press, 1986).

13. Ibid., 81.

14. "Souls at War," *Newsweek*, November 20, 1995, 59, quoted in Miller, *Discipling Nations*, 115 (see ch. 4, n. 1).

15. This chapter is not meant to get into all the global and political intrigues that have gone on in banking around the world; however there are some interesting things being written concerning banking systems such as the Federal Reserve. Let me just say this: It is not a federal, but a central bank, and not a reserve fund at all. For those interested in delving into this further, there are a number of books written on the subject of the Federal Reserve System, one of them being G. Edward Griffin's *The Creature from Jekyll Island* (Westlake Village, CA: American Media, 1994).

CHAPTER NINE

1. Cindy Jacobs, *Possessing the Gates of the Enemy* (Grand Rapids, MI: Chosen Books, 1991, 1994), 56.

2. James Goll, *The Lost Art of Intercession* (Shippensburg, PA: Destiny Image, 2007), 61.

3. There are some medieval-era theologians, such as Pseudo-Dionyisus in the fourth or fifth century, who propose that the thrones mentioned in this Daniel 7:9 passage referred to the Ezekiel 1:15-21 beings. These celestial beings are awesome in their powers and could be the "authorities" put in place over nations.

4. For more on this subject, please see my explanation in *Possessing the Gates of the Enemy*, 104-110.
5. Dutch Sheets, *Intercessory Prayer: How God Can Use Your Prayers to Move Heaven and Earth* (Ventura, CA: Regal Books, 1996), 57.
6. George Otis Jr.'s material can be obtained through his ministry, The Sentinel Group. His book *Informed Intercession: Transforming Your Community Through Spiritual Mapping and Strategic Prayer* (Ventura, CA: Renew, 1999) is an excellent manual on how to spiritually map an area.
7. It should be understood that you must not be involved in any known sin yourself when you begin this king of praying. Do not attempt it if you are, because you will only open yourself up to spiritual attack. For more information on this, see my book *Possessing the Gates of the Enemy*, particularly Chapter 3, "The Clean Heart Principle."
8. For more information on fasting, there are twenty-one references to it in *Possessing the Gates of the Enemy*.
9. The Homosexual Manifesto was entered into congressional records in 1987.
10. "Production Code," Wikipedia, the free encyclopedia, updated September 10, 2007, http://en.wikipedia.org/wiki/Hays_code (accessed September 12, 2007.

CHAPTER TEN

1. Dietrich Bonhoeffer, *The Cost of Discipleship* (New York, NY: Touchstone Publications, 1959, 1994), 17-18.
2. Eberhard Bethge, *Friendship and Resistance: Essays on Dietrich Bonhoeffer* (Grand Rapids, MI: Eerdmans Publishing Company, 1995), 19, quoted in "Review of Eberhard Bethge, Friendship and Resistance," The Bonhoefferian, June 16, 2007, http://dietrichbonhoeffer.com/2007/6/18/review-of-eberhard-bethge-friendship-and-resistance (accessed September 12, 2007).

3. Susan B. Anthony, who was arrested in the United States for voting when it was illegal for women to do so, quoted from the old Revoluntionary War maxim: "Resistance to tyranny is obedience to God."
4. Bonhoeffer, *The Cost of Discipleship*, 43.
5. Toby Mac and Michael Tait, with Wallbuilders, *Under God* (Minneapolis, MN: Bethany House Publishers, 2004), 21.
6. Jaeson Ma, *The Blueprint* (Ventura, CA: Regal Books, 2007), 174.
7. Charles G. Finney, *Freemasonry* (Brooklyn, NY: A & B Books Publishers, reprinted 1994), 65.
8. Schaeffer, *Christian Manifesto*, 66 (see ch. 6, n. 1).
9. Lucy G. Barber, *Marching to Washington* (Berkeley: University of California Press, 2002), 170-171.
10. A special note of thanks to Mary Jo Pierce for giving me this special gift one year for my birthday.
11. Harold Begbie, *The Life of General William Booth* (New York: The Macmillan Company, 1920), 107.
12. Rod Parsely, *Silent No More* (Lake Mary, FL: Charisma House, 2005), 1.

CHAPTER ELEVEN

1. Matthew Backholer, *Reformation to Revival* (Britain: By Faith Media, 2017), 9.
2. Notes received by email from David Thompson, vice-president of Transform Our World, March 1, 2021.
3. To find out where there are wells of revival in the United Kingdom, go to UKwells.org.
4. Backholer, *Reformation to Revival*, 144.
5. Rev. David Collier, quoted in Roy Jenkins, "The Welsh Revival," BBC.co.uk, Long-term consequences, June 16, 2009, https://www.bbc.co.uk/religion/religions/christianity/history/welshrevival_1.shtml (accessed May 30, 2021).
6. Backholer, *Reformation to Revival*, 145.

CHAPTER TWELVE

1. John Wesley, "The Letters of John Wesley, 1732," The Wesley Center Online, http://wesley.nnu.edu/john-wesley/the-letters-of-john-wesley/wesleys-letters-1732.

2. John Gillies, "Historical Collections of Accounts of Revival," quoted in Backholer, *Reformation to Revival*.

3. Eddie Hyatt, *The Great Prayer Awakening* (Grapevine, TX: Hyatt International Ministries, 2019), 4.

4. Ibid., 33-34.

5. Sean Smith, *I Am Your Sign* (Shippensburg, PA: Destiny Image, 2011), 20.

6. Keith Hardman, *The Spiritual Awakeners* (Chicago, IL: Moody Press, 1983), 2.

7. "Journal of the Continental Congress" (1907) 8,374, September 11, 1777, quoted in David and Tim Barton, *The American Story* (Aledo, TX: Wallbuilders Press, 2020), 187.

8. As stated earlier, I am not stating that the United States will be a theocracy during this dispensation. However, the heart and soul of our founders was turned to God. There simply was no separation of church and state. Rather, it was a separation of an established state church and the state.

9. This was taken from a Q&A session with George Otis from the Christian Union, www.tristateevoice.com.

10. Information sent me directly from George Otis Jr., *Journey to Transformation Beginner's Course* (The Sentinel Group).

11. Ibid.

12. Ed Silvoso, *Transformation* (Ventura, CA: Regal Books, 2007), 112.

13. Note: we want biblical justice as opposed to the term "social justice." Social justice can mean aborting babies and anti-biblical marriage practices, to name a few differences.

14. Silvoso, *Transformation,* 124.

15. H.B. Garlock and Ruthanne Garlock, *Before We Kill and Eat You* (Ventura, CA: Regal Books, 2006), 35.

16. Ibid., 74.

ABOUT CINDY JACOBS

CINDY JACOBS is a prophet, speaker, teacher, and author with a heart for discipling nations in the areas of prayer and the prophetic. She and Mike, her husband of 48 years, co-founded Generals International in 1985. They also founded the Reformation Prayer Network, which consists of a well-connected, fifty-state coalition of prayer leaders.

At nine years old, the Lord called Cindy when He urged her to read Psalm 2:8: *"Ask of me the nations for your inheritance, and the ends of the world for your possession."* That small seed God planted many years ago has sprouted and grown into an international ministry, taking Cindy to more than 100 nations of the world. She has spoken before hundreds of thousands, including many heads of nations. Some have called her the prophet to the presidents. Cindy helps people walk in the ministry of prophetic intercession, equipping them to pray effectively.

She has been recognized by *Charisma Magazine* as one of their "40 People Who Radically Changed Our World" and is listed in the *Who's Who Among American Women*. Cindy has also been recognized among the top 50 leaders in the world who are friends of Israel.

Cindy has written for *Charisma Magazine*, *Ministry Today*, and *Spirit-Led Woman* and is the author of eight books, including such bestsellers as *Possessing the Gates of the Enemy*, *The Voice of God*, and *Women Rise Up!* She is a frequent guest on many television shows.

In addition, she is the Chair of the Apostolic Council of Prophetic Elders, which has met together since 1999.

She and her husband, Mike, also convene the Global Prophetic Consultation with invited leaders from more than 65 nations.

She sits on the executive council for Empowered 21 and is an advisor to the boards of Christ for the Nations Bible Institute and Oral Roberts University. In 2019, Cindy joined the Board of Directors of Wagner University.

Cindy earned her B.A. in Music from Pepperdine University, Malibu, California, and also completed graduate work in Music from Pepperdine. She holds honorary doctorates from Asian Theological Association, for her work with unreached people groups, and from Christian International in Santa Rosa Beach, Florida. Cindy also received a third doctorate from Wagner University in Applied Theology in 2018.